HIDDEN CAMERAS

This book is for everyone who might use secret filming
to expose wrongdoing…and for everyone who supports
them, everyone who is affected by them and everyone who
is interested in them. In other words, it's for everyone.

HIDDEN CAMERAS

EVERYTHING YOU NEED TO KNOW ABOUT COVERT RECORDING, UNDERCOVER CAMERAS AND SECRET FILMING

Joe Plomin

Jessica Kingsley *Publishers*
London and Philadelphia

First published in 2016
by Jessica Kingsley Publishers
73 Collier Street
London N1 9BE, UK
and
400 Market Street, Suite 400
Philadelphia, PA 19106, USA

www.jkp.com

Library of Congress Cataloging in Publication Data
Plomin, Joe.
Hidden cameras : everything you need to know about
covert recording, undercover cameras and secret
filming / Joe Plomin.
pages cm
Includes bibliographical references.
ISBN 978-1-84905-643-4 (alk. paper)
1. Electronic surveillance. 2. Hidden camera photography.
3. Undercover operations. I. Title.
TK7882.E2P578 2015
621.36'7--dc23
2015024295

British Library Cataloguing in Publication Data
A CIP catalogue record for this book is available from the British Library.

ISBN 978 1 84905 643 4
eISBN 978 1 78450 136 5

Printed and bound in the United States

CONTENTS

ACKNOWLEDGEMENTS

Many kind and generous people have helped this book along. Special thanks are due to: Philip Abrams, Malcolm Balen, Kevin Biderman, Joe Casey, Eileen Chubb, Roger Courtiour, Sheila Cracknell, John Davison, Clive Edwards, Jim Gray, Andrew Head, James Hellings, John Hession, Alison Holt, Wendy Inchley, Roger Law, Roger Mahony, Mandy Mugford, Robert Plomin, Tamanna Rahman, Joshua Sallon, Russell Sharp, Frank Simmonds, Ceri Thomas, Karen Wightman, Joyce Zannoni, numerous necessarily anonymous whistle-blowers, and finally, most importantly, the two ladies who believed in this book even when I've been at my most annoying: Jessica and Esther. Thank you all. Please forgive me, anyone I've left off who helped me out...

PHOTO CREDITS

INTRODUCTION

Secret filming is no longer the preserve of a small cabal of professional journalists and private investigators. Social activists, citizen journalists and watchful members of the public are now recording more covert footage, and more important evidence, than professionals like journalists, private investigators and others. The general public itself is using cameras to stop illegal or antisocial behaviour.

They need help with that covert recording – they could often do it better. People across the UK email me at the BBC's *Panorama* programme, where I work, with secret footage and audio recordings hoping we can broadcast their evidence. Currently, most of what we are sent does not prove what the sender hopes to prove. That can be because of technical issues (for example, the quality is too poor), but more often it is because someone has not sufficiently questioned why they are recording or what their footage means.

There is a second group of people whose mistakes I see when I go through the BBC's *Panorama* postbag and who can also benefit from the window I am trying to open into the reality of covert recording. Police officers, social workers, media broadcasters, politicians, print journalists, as well as regulators and their inspectors too often respond poorly to secret footage. Professionals can fail to assess and interpret secret footage properly and therefore can benefit from the advice in this book.

This book contains all of the strategies, techniques and observations from the time I have spent working with hidden cameras, since 2002. I hope that sharing them will assist more people to get it right.

THE INSPECTOR'S STORY

A regional manager (whom I won't name) for the national health and social care inspectorate of England, the Care Quality Commission (CQC), spent an entire day with me at the BBC's headquarters in Central London in 2014.

She was very polite and extremely diligent, but when she first arrived I felt something slightly odd was going on; it was hard to pinpoint exactly what, though.

The CQC had contacted me regarding one of the films I had produced, during the making of which reporter and journalist Alex Lee worked in a large elderly care home as a care worker. The care home did not realise at the time that Alex was also wearing hidden cameras and working as a journalist for the BBC.

Alex had filmed evidence of poor care being given in that facility – even one care worker apparently slapping a resident.[1]

The CQC came to me after the film was broadcast saying they wanted to ensure there were no further issues that they needed to understand related to the home. They said they wanted to get 'more insight into the way care is provided' in order to 'help us get to the right action quickly'.

When she first arrived, though, this regional manager seemed a bit distant. To my discredit, I assumed – wrongly, as it turned out – that maybe she had been ordered to come see me, that maybe she was reluctant and uninterested.

But that was not the problem at all.

She spoke to me at length and worked through the detail of what we had found and how we had uncovered it. She worked hard the whole day. This clearly was not someone who was reluctant. The more time that passed, the warmer she got – and she wasn't doing any of this simply to please me.

She finally cleared up the mystery of what was going on.

At the end of the day, just before she was about to go, she admitted that when she first turned up she had a settled opinion about hidden cameras: she just didn't like secret filming.

She came to the BBC convinced that hidden cameras were a bad idea, full stop. Now, instead, she was struck by the depth of understanding we had achieved in really very few shifts working in an elderly care home. She told me she now saw that we, during our investigation, had clearly agonised about everything we did throughout our filming.

I worry about putting words in her mouth, but it seems to me that across the day she spent with me she came to understand that all secret filming is not equal, that some of it is more worthwhile – if it is done well.

This care home's real culture had been closed off and hidden away, even to inspectors during inspections. However, the people living there – who were too often voiceless or misunderstood – and the people working there, like our undercover reporter, could see what was really happening.[2]

No one should be against secret filming if it is done properly. Equally, no one should be in favour of secret filming if it is done badly or unethically.

Once professionals who are involved with secret filming understand it better, they can take a more nuanced approach and identify – as I try to do every time I go through *Panorama*'s email inbox – which secret recordings need the most attention and action.

There has too often been a fake battle going on between those 'in favour of secret filming' and those 'against it'. We need a more informed and nuanced discussion. One could well argue that proportionate and effective covert recording of antisocial or illegal behaviour should be supported by everyone, whereas indiscriminate invasion of privacy should be avoided and even excoriated. How we can inculcate good filming practices, and how to judge that distinction, is the real challenge.

In June 2015, the Royal College of Nursing's conference passed a resolution to oppose covert surveillance. Referring to why nurses were so worried about the cameras, Dr Peter Carter, Chief Executive of the RCN, said: 'I can understand why. You are doing a job feeling like you are constantly under the microscope. It's not a panacea to cure all problems of abuse.'[3]

Nurses at the College's Bournemouth conference were reportedly told that concerns should be raised with managers instead, and were warned that footage could be inappropriately posted on social media and Twitter.

Those concerns – namely, being under the microscope, whether concerns could be resolved by complaints instead of surveillance and how any footage collected is used – are valid, sensible and reasonable. I am agreeing that those really are problems, despite being one of the country's foremost practitioners of secret filming.

Here's the thing though: none of that is an argument against people doing secret filming, *per se*. None of those points justify banning people from covert recording. The Royal College of Nursing really just pointed out why secret filming needs to be carefully considered, managed and justified.[4]

A more considered and balanced argument was advanced by Caroline Abrahams, Charity Director at Age UK, who said:

> Cameras should only be used when there is good reason to suspect abuse and neglect. Every older person has a right to privacy and dignity and as most people receiving care need help with intimate personal tasks, including washing and dressing, cameras must be fully justifiable and carefully balance the rights of older people to live their lives free from surveillance. Where possible cameras should only be used with the consent of the resident, and footage should be treated as the property of the resident or their representatives, not of the home.[5]

The toothpaste will not go back in the tube – nurses cannot prevent technology changing their world any more than police officers, security guards, nannies, doctors and other have been able to in the past.

There is a revolution going on among people desperate to find out the truth about how their loved ones are being treated or another social ill. People are deciding that they will not wait any longer and that they will no longer tolerate being brushed off.

People are not accepting not knowing any longer.

People are taking matters into their own hands.

THE STRUCTURE OF THIS BOOK

This book takes a narrative approach to the story of secret filming and assisting people in future with doing it or understanding it. In addition to providing eight chapters that contain specific instruction and advice, I also try to immerse the reader in the experience of covert investigation by offering 'Undercover Tales' – real-world stories of real undercover filming.

This is not a textbook; it is a guidebook, a journey into a world that for most people feels unusual and sometimes even impossible when they first step into it but which is really just our ordinary world magnified through a tiny hidden lens.

The eight main chapters cover the history of secret filming, technical advice on using proper cameras and then on using the cameras in phones, ethical guidance, the legal context, the emotional and physical costs, what to do with the footage and predictions for the future.

Chapter 1 tells a potted history of journalistic infiltration, of secret recording and covert technology.

Chapter 2 provides specific guidance on 'proper' secret cameras and how to avoid some common mistakes. This is a step-by-step guide for choosing a camera, installing it, using it and safely retrieving the covert footage.

Chapter 3 is a guide to using a mobile or cellular telephone to film people secretly and safely: 'secretly' in that if someone doesn't realise they are being filmed, then the recording is 'covert', and 'safely' because phones are risky – they are obviously more visible than 'proper' hidden cameras. Phones with integrated cameras are powerful tools for social justice but can put people in danger.

Chapter 4 sets out the ethical considerations which, I would argue, should be thought through *before* and *during* any secret filming.

Chapter 5 provides a 'beginner's guide' to the legal questions involved with covert recording.

Chapter 6 describes two issues that often take people by surprise and then offers advice on how to cope with them. These issues are essentially the logistical difficulties involved in doing secret filming well and the emotional costs involved with deception and recording people without their knowledge.

Chapter 7 sets out what happens after the secret camera or mobile phone camera stops filming. This chapter breaks down step by step the choices for people who have done secret filming and for people presented with their footage.

Finally, Chapter 8 looks to the future, describing the likely technological developments in covert recording that will occur over the next decade – and considers the implications for all of us.

TERMINOLOGY

There is more detail on the types of covert recording and the differences between them in Chapters 2 and 3, but it is appropriate to provide a preliminary guide to the meanings of certain key terms. I use 'covert recording' and 'secret filming' interchangeably to cover all occasions where someone films someone else without their knowledge, whether that is with a 'proper' secret camera or with a camera in a phone.

'Hidden cameras' are recording devices in which a camera and recorder have been deliberately *disguised*. Some secret filming is done with the cameras of mobile or cellular phones.

NOTES

1. Holt, A. (2014) 'Staff sacking and suspensions over poor elderly care.' Available at www.bbc.co.uk/news/uk-27128011, accessed on 3 April 2015.

2. The care home in question says they have 'invested hundreds of thousands of pounds in a programme to overhaul care, equipment, facilities, decor and staff training'. See Robinson, E. (2015) 'The Old Deanery rebranded as the New Deanery as new owners invest hundreds of thousands of pounds.' Available at www.braintreeandwithamtimes. co.uk/news/12903163.The_Old_Deanery_rebranded_as_the_ New_Deanery_as_new_owners_invest_hundreds_of_thousands_of_ pounds, accessed on 10 May 2015.

3. Borland, S. and Sinmaz, E. (2015) '"Ban worried relatives from filming the elderly in care homes," argue nurses who "don't want to be scrutinised".' *Daily Mail*, 22 June. Available at www.dailymail.co.uk/health/article-3134928/Ban-worried-relatives-filming-elderly-care-homes-argue-nurses-don-t-want-scrutinised.html, accessed on 4 July 2015.

4. There is more detail on specifically how and why that can be done in later chapters (particularly Chapter 4).

5. Gregory, A. (2015) 'Nurses want spy cameras banned from care homes due to "remote supervision" fears.' *Daily Mirror*, 22 June. Available at www.mirror.co.uk/news/uk-news/nurses-want-spy-cameras-banned-5931165, accessed 4 July 2015.

UNDERCOVER TALES

First Going Undercover

The night before I began my first long-term undercover assignment, my nerves were tangled. Since then I've never felt as frightened as I felt that night. I felt so worried that I was somehow numbed, distanced from myself and what was in front of me. After all, someone taking up secret cameras could prevent harm, but they could also be caught and reprimanded, or even worse. It is always a nerve-wracking experience.

I was going to begin working inside an animal sanctuary the next morning, while also covertly filming. I would have to go about my business as a volunteer sweeping out bird poo from cages and feeding animals, but I would also be secretly filming some of the people around me, without them realising. Our aim was to expose evidence that some people were mistreating animals and even killing healthy birds.[1]

It was a warm spring night. I was just 24 years old. I had driven my more-rusty-than-red second-hand car over to my then-girlfriend's house. I needed to be somewhere quiet, I needed to not talk. I was trying to avoid thinking too much. Really, I was hoping that I would not screw up and that my head would not explode with worry.

I shut the curtains of her Dorset bungalow's front room. I pushed the tablecloth back off the dining table and put down a hard suitcase, a moulded-plastic black box with a handle. My girlfriend walked in asking why her house was pitch black while the sun was still out. I was just worried that the retired – and nosey – neighbours would look in and see the camera.

I unfastened the clasps on the box and opened the lid. Inside was a secret camera. The main piece was just an ordinary big and bulky handicam, the type of camera a tourist might carry, but it also had a black cable attached to it. That black lead was the clever bit: it ran to a miniature camera lens. That lens was hidden in a T-shirt such that it could point out and film from my chest without anyone realising.

It was exciting but foreign and slightly unbelievable. Could I really get away with wearing this big thing?

Would no one realise I was filming them? Really?

I took out the camera, carefully handling its leads and strapping them on. I taped down any spare extension to my chest and tried not to think about the tape ripping off my chest hairs when I finished my day's work.

Check the whole thing is hidden.

Check the camera is working 16 times more before you leave the room.

Come back into the room and check again.

Breathe. Relax. Remember the rules. Remember the lies you told last time.

It is a fear that never goes away. It comes with a pulse of adrenaline. When you are using a secret camera, it becomes an inescapable presence in everything you do, whether you are wearing it or leaving it in a room. You do not just switch on the camera. It is a two-way street. While the secret camera is there, you are aware of it, you think of it — you are switched on too.

Looking in the mirror, every bulge and every bump is so obvious it screams out, 'Hey, this guy is an undercover reporter!' You sweat. Then you go in...to try to change things.

In the years since then, cameras have become miniaturised and much cheaper. The little cottage industry I worked in, where journalists were doing most of the covert recording that ended up in newspapers and on televisions, has been swept away or at least lost its importance.

Journalists still use hidden cameras, but members of the public are now recording most of the secret footage that is being broadcast in news reports every week all over the world.

It appears my breed, the journalists and professionals, is passing the baton to ordinary people.

THE TRANSITION FROM UNDERCOVER REPORTER TO UNDERCOVER PRODUCER

During the course of a dozen investigations, I captured evidence of antisocial or illegal behaviour by wearing secret recording equipment. The footage I personally filmed was broadcast on national or local television in the UK, mainly at the BBC. Then, about ten years ago, I hung up my secret camera and began managing other undercover reporters.

One of those journalists was Joe Casey, a Kilkenny-born but West London-raised Irishman, proud of his heritage and determined to have a positive influence on the world. He is gifted with a strong heart. He is passionate about doing good for others.

I hired Joe to work undercover, to wear cameras and infiltrate a private hospital on the outskirts of Bristol which was supposed to care for vulnerable people with learning disabilities or autism and challenging behaviour. That hospital was Winterbourne View.

During just 14 shifts undercover on the top floor of that hospital, Joe filmed patients being slapped, goaded, kicked and tormented by some of the people who were paid to care for them.

Unusually (and usefully for us), Joe's sense of social duty is hidden by a tough exterior: unless he deliberately lets on, it is very easy to assume he is 'one of the boys'. When Joe went undercover, pretending to be just another care worker, none of the people around him got any hint he was concerned about anything. Although he endured some of the most difficult and challenging experiences any undercover reporter has faced, to onlookers at the hospital he looked like any other careless guy more worried about his day off than what was going on.

Everyone around him thought that he was 'one of them'.

To keep down costs, I had rented an unfurnished house. Joe and I slept on mattresses on the floor. I borrowed chairs from the landlady. With a folding chair each, in the evening we would quickly eat the food I had prepared, plates on our laps, living like ascetics and avoiding the neighbours – our lives focused entirely on the evidence we were gathering.

After every 12-hour shift working at Winterbourne View Hospital, Joe still had another several hours of work to do, just to download, back up and review the footage he had filmed, to make notes on what he had seen and to film video diaries.

Although my duty was less 'glamorous', less important and less dangerous, I had more than a day's work between each of his shifts at the hospital, just watching everything, checking every frame and ensuring we knew exactly what he was seeing but also what he was doing, so that I could provide constant feedback.

It was an intense and surreal existence for both of us.

Looking back, I think that intensity distanced us from what we were seeing in a way that made the investigation possible. The horrors that were unfolding in front of me on my laptop were of a pace and severity that could have been intolerable for a two-man team with no relief.[2]

A Minister of State in the Department of Health, Norman Lamb MP (Member of Parliament), told the British Parliament:

> The scandal that unfolded at Winterbourne View was devastating. We were all rightly shocked, angered and dismayed by the appalling abuse uncovered by the *Panorama* programme in May 2011...
>
> The abuse at Winterbourne View was criminal. Staff whose job was to care for people instead routinely mistreated and abused them. Management allowed a culture of abuse to flourish. Warning signs were not picked up by health or local authorities, the residents' families were not listened to, and the concerns raised by a whistleblower went unheeded. The fact that it took a television documentary to raise the alarm speaks volumes.[3]

That hospital was licensed to provide only assessment and treatment. Instead of fulfilling that purpose, many of the patients ended up languishing there for years. Particularly on the top floor, Winterbourne View had become a place where vulnerable people were not assessed and not treated – just incarcerated and, sometimes, mistreated terribly. I later wrote the following about the film captured by Joe:

> None of this abuse and mistreatment would have been revealed were it not for events back in 2011, when I drove down with Joe Casey – our undercover reporter who actually worked at Winterbourne View Hospital – to start work. I was there to manage him, manage the investigation and to keep an eye on his footage.

The hospital was shut as a result of our investigation. Eleven people were convicted for crimes of neglect or common assault. Since that film, the Criminal Justice and Courts Act 2015 has been enacted. That Act created new offences of corporate neglect and corporate ill treatment – we are told that it could (if enforced) mean owners and providers are prosecuted for failings in their institutions.

Secret filming can lift whole houses off the ground. It can prevent harm, and it can be good.

NOTES

1. See BBC Inside Out (2003) 'Animal sanctuary exposed.' Available at www.bbc.co.uk/insideout/south/series3/animal_sanctuary_exposed. shtml, accessed on 25 April 2015. At the time of broadcast, the owner denied the allegations and said in a statement that the sanctuary had recently passed its zoo inspection and that this negates some of the allegations. However, the owner was later found guilty of wildlife offences; see BBC News (2004) 'Owl boss pays for wildlife crime.' Available at http://news.bbc.co.uk/1/hi/england/ hampshire/3719158.stm, accessed on 25 April 2015.

2. Plomin, J. (2013) 'The abuse of vulnerable adults at Winterbourne View Hospital: the lessons to be learned.' *Journal of Adult Protection 15*, 4, 182–191.

3. Lamb, N. (2012) 'Statement on final report into Winterbourne View.' Available at www.parliament.uk/business/news/2012/december/ statement-on-final-report-into-winterbourne-view, accessed on 24 January 2015.

Chapter 1

HOW DID WE GET HERE?

The History of Infiltration and Covert Recording

The era of the professional undercover journalist wearing tiny cameras in order to expose wrongdoing reached its peak in 2009. There was a lot of anger that year. In April, just 6 months after the world economy was shredded by the lies and games of bankers (and by the rest of us taking unsustainable house and personal loans),[1] that anger found its expression and epicentre in London.

Thousands of people gathered on the streets there in order to protest at the forum of the governments and central bank governors from the 20 major economies or 'G20'. Many of the people who came to protest wore black clothes, and some had handkerchiefs over their faces. The police wore riot helmets and shields, and massed together. The focus of it all was the City of London (the main financial district), and particularly the big banks' international headquarters, towering over the skyline.

G20 crowd and police lines

Seething masses of humanity and walls of police mixed on the streets with journalists and cameras. Many of those cameras were waved openly at people, but some of the filming was less obvious – because it was being done secretly.

More covert recording was going on in one day, and in one place, than ever before. The City of London's streets were crawling with hidden cameras. I had never seen such a deployment of infiltration on all sides. Undercover journalists mixed among the protestors. Plain-clothes police were out in force too, I was told, including a number of officers with surveillance cameras trained on protestors – recording faces and identities.

G20 injured protestor and police

The conflict seemed preordained and almost rehearsed from previous protests. The police had said they would not tolerate anarchy or violence, and the protestors had said they would be peaceful. Journalists were seeking to record and judge who was right. They had been seeking out black-hooded anarchists planning to attend and who were allegedly intent on violence.

It was the high-water mark for secret recording both by the state and by journalists. I suspect that never again will so many undercover cameras be in use *by paid professionals* in one place. However, despite that massive effort on both sides, they all missed the main confrontation.

The abiding image of that conflict is of Ian Tomlinson, a newspaper vendor trying to make his way home through the edge of those protests when he was pushed and struck – causing his death. Tomlinson had not been involved with the protests. He was just trying to get home.

An American banker, a portfolio manager named Christopher La Jaunie, happened to be on that side street where Tomlinson was attacked and happened to have a compact digital camera.[2] Mr La Jaunie filmed those iconic images of Mr Tomlinson being struck, using that camera at a distance, unseen.

The omnipresent camera in everyone's mobile or cellular phones, at the ready in every pocket – or in this case, a tourist camera – could turn anyone, even a passing banker at an anti-banker protest, into a citizen journalist. La Jaunie's recording changed the face of the G20 riots. That footage forced the Metropolitan Police to respond properly to the tragic death. The police officer who pushed over Mr Tomlinson was acquitted of manslaughter but sacked for gross misconduct. The Met made a formal apology to the family and paid an out-of-court settlement.[3]

The tectonic plates that govern who films who shifted at that moment. The basic assumptions about how secret filming is done truly changed. It became much clearer to me than ever before that, in future, professionals like myself would no longer be doing most of the covert work and surveillance that appeared on television and in films. We had handed over that responsibility to a new generation: citizen journalists.

Journalists were all following what they thought was the 'big story' – that is, the main bulk of protestors and particularly the anarchists in black with bandanas hiding their faces. The police were focused on the same group, trying to identify the ringleaders. All those professional cameras were clumped together, pointing where everyone expected the main action to occur. In other words, none of the professionals – the police, the investigators, the journalists – were on the little side street where Ian Tomlinson died.

It is generally a fact that members of the public employ surveillance either more indiscriminately (outside their homes, in their cars or on their bikes, for example) or else more reactively (seeing something bad and switching their phone on) than professionals. That means they can react and record in places where professionals are nowhere to be seen. Real people are able to record important evidence that journalists could not even dream of getting close enough to capture.

This chapter sets out a condensed history of some of the reasons we have arrived at this position. It is just a brief and selective history, more of a flavour than a definitive guide.[4]

The short summary would be that in the second half of the nineteenth century covert cameras were invented and followed by hidden audio recorders. After the first proper secret filming took place, undercover television was invented. Then citizen journalists, social activists and others took up video cameras. And now the public is using 'proper' secret cameras.

THE BIRTH OF SECRETLY RECORDED IMAGES

The history of hidden cameras and covert recording is driven by the story of ordinary filming – that is, open recording with normal cameras. The two things run in tandem. As long as there has been a way to record things, someone somewhere has been thinking about using that same technology to capture secret footage without the subject realising.

This truth goes right back to the beginning: it was not that long after the photographic stills camera was invented that someone started thinking about how to make a *secret* stills camera.

The result was the 'Lancaster', a covert camera pocket watch. This was a palm-sized fob watch – obviously not something on one's wrist back in Victorian days.

Lancaster Pocket Watch, patented 1886[5]
Source: Copyright © Bonhams

The idea was that anyone could play spy and take photos of anyone else with a truly hidden camera.

The Lancaster looked like a pocket watch until the time came to take a photograph, when it was unlatched, extended and the device was activated.

The problem is that the Lancaster was really impractical. A camera specialist at Bonhams auction house said:

> It would have been very inconvenient to use as four very small catches had to be released in order to remove the glass screen and to fit a separate metal

sensitised material holder for each exposure. As a result, the model sadly sold badly and is much rarer than the improved version which came on the market in 1890.[6]

Other hidden stills cameras were developed across the next 50 years.[7]

Most of the covert images taken between the 1890s and 1940s did *not* use a proper hidden stills camera like the Lancaster. Most of the photos being taken without the subject realising during that time used a long-lens camera – the photography was hidden by dint of being at a distance.

For example, in the 1870s the British state used long-lens stills cameras to gather pictures of suffragettes, women who had been imprisoned for demanding women's voting rights. Because the police photographers were far away, the suffragettes did not realise their image was being captured. In 2003, Kew Gardens held an exhibit of those surveillance photographs. They appear almost paparazzi to modern eyes.[8]

Women seeking the right to vote are captured, in moments of rest, in those photos without their knowledge.

Today, the position is actually very similar to back then: secret filming is now being done both with 'proper' secret cameras (the modern heirs to the Lancaster) and also with the cameras in ordinary mobile or cellular telephones (just as ordinary cameras were being used back then).

Although there have been 'proper' hidden cameras since not long after the birth of photography, most covert recording has always used ordinary cameras that are perfectly visible but hidden far away or used such that no one sees them.

THE HIDDEN AUDIO RECORDER

Audio recorders lent themselves to disguise more easily than early stills cameras. Tape recorders changed from being large reel-to-reel devices into machines that were small enough to fit in a briefcase – and were then used to capture serious evidence of wrongdoing or antisocial behaviour.

The era of the true secret recording had begun.

The following example illustrates the reach of an audio recorder, hidden away, anywhere and in anything where it will fit. In 1976, two journalists, Barrie Penrose and Roger Courtiour, snuck a tape recorder hidden in a briefcase into meetings with the British prime minister, Harold Wilson, just weeks after he had quit office.[9]

In remarkable tape recordings the former prime minister set out his fears that the British Secret Service believed he was a Communist spy. Decades later, declassified documents would prove Wilson largely right: there was a plot against him led by his own spies. Penrose wrote the following:

> Unbeknown to Wilson, Courtiour and I secretly recorded many of our meetings with him, almost always conducted at his Georgian house at 5 Lord North Street, close to the House of Commons. The cumbersome machine was smuggled into his study in a briefcase carried by Courtiour. Over a period of nine months we accumulated hours of tape recordings. Those tapes have, since then, remained untouched in the loft of my Kent home and at Courtiour's London home.[10]

There are other examples where audio recorders changed whole sectors in just the same ways that secret cameras are now opening up new hidden worlds.

In 1972, *The Guardian* newspaper in England used a disguised audio recorder to prove an ex-convict was being blackmailed by two police detectives in an effort to make him name other criminals. They had set him up – made it look as if he'd committed a crime they knew he'd had no part in:

DETECTIVE:	But I don't particularly want to lock you up, but I want someone.
MAN:	So in exchange for me...
DETECTIVE:	I want someone.[11]

Covert audio recording technology meant that journalists at the BBC, *The Guardian* and elsewhere could absolutely prove the wrongdoing by public officials in a way that previous generations would have struggled with just pen and paper based only on testimony.

THE FIRST SECRET FILMING: AUDIO, AND IMAGES AT A DISTANCE

Roger Courtiour was not just someone who recorded a former prime minister secretly with a hidden audio recorder; he was also one of the first people to do actual proper secret filming, using film cameras.

'This was the early seventies', he told me. 'There were only maybe five or six places people sold drugs around London. We learned about one and I went in to buy drugs wearing an audio recorder while the team filmed me using a long lens on a camera, from a vehicle parked nearby.'

It sounds easy enough, but Roger remembers that it was actually anything but straightforward: 'Of course being me, the audio recorder I was wearing didn't work. I don't think it switched on. We were [just] learning everything back then.'

We only see examples of secret filming that works, but often people fail because of technical problems. Today the same remains true. Members of the public doing their own secret filming need to do secret filming better in order to avoid being caught and in order to capture footage that proves the allegations they are making, just like back when journalists were learning the tricks of the trade.

Most of those lessons appear in later chapters, but one seems appropriate to discuss here because Roger talked about it when he reminisced about that first time he used secret filming. That lesson is that there are real limits to secret filming. There are many things that covert recorders cannot capture. Roger was filming drug deals, and at the time that seemed to him to be the end of the matter. He thought about it in pretty straightforward terms: 'It was illegal, so of course it seemed like something we should film.'

Now he thinks more about the fact that his secret filming could only tackle certain targets. 'Later I thought more about the fact that we were filming low-level people, not the people making the real money,' he said. He could film anything at the street level with the new long-lens film cameras while wearing an audio recorder, but his cameras could never get at the bosses. Secret filming is very powerful, but there are always limits to what it can capture. As with most of the lessons in this book, that is just a fact that needs to be borne in mind and considered in each case of covert recording.

REAL UNDERCOVER TELEVISION

In the decades that followed, the camera crept ever closer to the action in television documentaries. Television recording started (as above in Roger Courtiour's recollection) with audio recorders in someone's pocket and giant film cameras some distance off. Then cameras just small enough to fit in a lady's handbag or similar were developed. Finally, recorders – audio and picture – became small enough for operatives to wear in their clothes.

Early covert recording technology was terribly bulky and unwieldy. Undercover reporters working for me these days still worry they will be discovered even though their recorders are tiny, but when I started out just 15 years ago I had a quite bulky tourist-style video camera under my armpit. With some pretty clever modification, a cable could run off and take in video and audio from external microphones and a camera lens.

That modification, attaching a remote tiny lens, brought both image and sound right on top of the action. We could record wrongdoing while working just so long as no one spotted the giant recorder.

Those newly modified cameras were beyond the scope, expense and knowledge of most of the public at that time. The fact that we had these things and that most people could not get access to them meant that for a while the story of secret filming felt like it was pretty much the story of journalists. The need for specialist cameras gave birth to a mini-industry of which I am at the tail end.

Many British readers will remember the long-running ITV series *World in Action*, which is credited with pioneering the use of covert cameras in a series of documentaries:

World in Action, an investigative current affairs series from Granada Television (1963–98), used these methods [of undercover filming] successfully where ordinary entry was impossible and where there was demonstrable public interest justification. To enter a guarded steel works where over ten workers had died in industrial accidents, this writer [Gavin MacFadyen] impersonated a local iron worker secretly to film where and how these workers had died. In other undercover films, on corruption and child labour in Hong Kong, he impersonated a Catholic priest from the Holy Carpenter Guest House, and an Indiana doll salesman. Later he would play right wing American television producer while documenting election fraud by the People's National Congress in Guyana. Other producers secretly filmed while pretending to be anthropologists in Argentina while pursuing Nazi war criminals, and conventional tourists while investigating Czechoslovakia during the Cold War...[12]

Another *World in Action* film is particularly relevant to people carrying out their own secret filming today. In 1997, the team rigged an entire domestic home with hidden cameras. That technique, putting cameras in objects that then sit static inside a room, is the one we now see members of the public using most, whether it is in care homes, hospitals, when filming a nanny or even when catching a philandering spouse. Before such techniques came into wider circulation, journalists had invented them for television.

It was not just *World in Action* that drove through the use of secret cameras as a tool to capture evidence of antisocial or illegal behaviour. There were many other British TV series that used covert recording, programmes such as *Kenyon Confronts* (BBC), *Undercover Britain* (Channel 4) and *Disguises* (ITV).

There are more undercover television series and documentaries than I could list here. The point is that journalists have played a substantial role in the evolution of covert cameras; we have learned some lessons about what works and what does not work. I am trying to pass those lessons on to a new generation of covert photographers and videographers.

CITIZEN JOURNALISM BEFORE UNDERCOVER CAMERAS: ARMED WITH TOURIST CAMERAS

The first wave of citizen video journalism was powered not by hidden cameras but instead by the public using 8-mm and SVHS cameras to film events the mainstream media ignored. The sheer availability of those relatively small 8-mm and SVHS cameras made it possible for almost anyone to get a camera and record what they believed was important, rather than what some news editor decided to send a camera crew out to record.

'You could now go into a shop in Bradford, Brisbane or Birmingham, Alabama, hand over the equivalent of $1,000 and have yourself an almost broadcast-quality camcorder kit', Thomas Harding wrote of that video revolution.[13]

The existence of tourist cameras and video activism from the 1980s onwards produced worries about privacy. Hemmed in on one side by surveillance by the state and on the other by widespread filming by individuals, there was concern from some professionals that nothing would be private.

One leading video activist and later prolific Sky News journalist, Roddy Mansfield, wrote in Harding's book:

> Some people express concern that an army of activists wielding camcorders increases society's 'Big Brother' factor. Yet if you attend live exports or sabotaging a hunt, you'll be videoed by the police, private security guards and detective agencies working for the government, all of whom are compiling secret files on us. That's spying on people. Yet when I see a security guard assault someone, or a police officer use unreasonable force, or a fox being torn apart, or a 400-year-old tree being destroyed, I'll be the first one to video it. That's not spying on people; that's justice![14]

Taking up cameras always takes bravery.

Those tourist cameras wielded by citizen journalists were not 'secret cameras'; they were not hidden. They did still sometimes record important footage, where the subject of filming did not realise. The most famous early covert footage – filmed by an ordinary citizen – was the beating of Rodney King by a group of police officers in 1992, in Los Angeles. That footage was covert because the police officers did not realise they were being filmed; they did not know someone on a balcony had a zoom on a small tourist camera powerful enough to capture evidence of that beating from a significant distance.

WHERE WE HAVE ARRIVED: THE CITIZEN JOURNALIST AND HIDDEN CAMERAS

Now it is not going to be people like me who sweat most and really change things. The most interesting secret filming is increasingly not being done by professional journalists. Members of the public are taking up the baton.

In 2012, Joyce Zannoni was disgusted by what her mother was being fed in a care home in Leicestershire. Her mother was supposed to have only liquidised foods, but she had been served beans on toast. On another occasion, her mother's window was broken and the ceiling was mouldy. It was clear that her mother was not being properly cared for.

The grand-looking house on the hill at the top of a pretty village, with its high stone wall and open garden, was not matching its exterior with good care inside – at least as far as Joyce could tell.

Completely disgruntled, Joyce took up her mobile phone and used it to film what she was seeing. The mobile phone in Joyce's pocket had – in one fell swoop – turned into a weapon against poor care. It had turned into a method of gathering evidence. She captured hard proof that backed up her concerns.

At that stage, like most members of the public using their phone or a hidden camera to secretly record wrongdoing, she had no thought that the footage she was recording might be featured in a television programme on the BBC's *Panorama* programme. That was not her purpose. She just wanted her mother to be given food she could eat.

Joyce's phone was visible, but it captured what was really happening, without people realising, at least at first. On the footage you can hear when a care worker spots her and tells her she has to stop filming, that she is not allowed to film in the care home. Joyce has to stop – she has been discovered. Although it was not very surreptitious, it *was* covert filming in order to uncover evidence of wrongdoing until she was discovered.

Mobile or cell phone cameras are becoming an important tool for gathering evidence.

Joyce's evidence prompted the council to investigate. They substantiated her concerns 'under the category of neglect'. Their own investigators – coming in as a result of her evidence and persistence – found chaotic mealtimes and serious environmental concerns.

Later, we got involved and some of Joyce's footage and her photos were broadcast on the BBC.

In response to the film (which I produced), and despite the council's findings, the care home denied that some residents missed out on food and drink. They did not accept there was neglect and have pointed out that, since the film, an inquest into the death of Joyce's mother did not conclude that neglect had been a contributing factor.

The owner of the care home also formally complained to the UK broadcast regulator, Ofcom, about that film, arguing that we were unfair. Those complaints were not upheld.[15]

Joyce's footage and photos, combined with her incredibly diligent note-taking – she had kept all the relevant emails, dates and notes from that time – had won the day.

This example is only one of many from around the world.

The reach of miniature cameras will only increase over the coming decades.

They need to be used wisely.

NOTES

1. The Economist (2013) 'The origins of the financial crisis.' Available at www.economist.com/news/schoolsbrief/21584534-effects-financial-crisis-are-still-being-felt-five-years-article, accessed on 1 February 2015.

2. This has sometimes been questioned, primarily by conspiracy theorists; however, see contemporaneous report for Tomlinson's inquest: www.bbc.co.uk/news/uk-12856002, accessed on 19 November 2015.

3. Lewis, P. (2009) 'Video reveals G20 police assault on man who died.' Available at www.theguardian.com/uk/2009/apr/07/video-g20-police-assault, accessed on 5 June 2014.

4. Readers who want more on the history, particularly of investigative journalism, are referred to: de Burgh, H. (2008) *Investigative Journalism*. Oxford: Routledge; or Pilger, J. (2004) *Tell Me No Lies*. London: Jonathan Cape.

5. See, for example, Thomas, R. (2011) 'The history and evolution of spy and investigative photography.' Available at www.pimall.com/nais/nl/spyphotography.html, accessed on 1 February 2015; or http://io9.com/5959454/steampunk-spy-fi-real-life-gadgets-perfect-for-a-victorian-era-james-bond, accessed on 19 November 2015.

6. The Watchismo Times (2007) 'Victorian 1886 spy camera pocket watch.' Available at http://watchismo.blogspot.co.uk/2007/05/watchismo-times_10.html, accessed on 4 April 2015.

7. Stapley, J. (2014) '6 of the best vintage spy cameras ever made.' Available at www.amateurphotographer.co.uk/latest/articles/6-of-the-best-vintage-spy-cameras-ever-made-5475, accessed on 4 April 2015.

8. Casciani, D. (2003) 'Spy pictures of suffragettes revealed.' Available at http://news.bbc.co.uk/1/hi/magazine/3153024.stm, accessed on 24 July 2015.

9. Dwyer, P. (2006) The Plot Against Harold Wilson. British Broadcasting Company, BBC2, 2006. London: British Broadcasting Company [no longer available online]. Also: Wheeler, B. (2006) 'Wilson "plot": the secret tapes.' Available at http://news.bbc.co.uk/1/hi/uk_politics/4789060.stm, accessed on 5 June 2014.

10. Penrose, B. (2006) Quoted in Wheeler, B. (2006) 'Wilson "plot": the secret tapes.' Available at http://news.bbc.co.uk/1/hi/uk_politics/4789060.stm, accessed on 5 June 2014.

11. Bunyan, T. (1976) *The History and Practice of the Political Police in Britain* (p.220). London: Julian Friedmann Publishers.

12. MacFadyen, G. (2008) The Practices of Investigative Journalism. In H. de Burgh (ed.) *Investigative Journalism* (p.150). Oxford: Routledge.

13. Harding, T. (ed.) (2001) *The Video Activist Handbook* (2nd ed.) (p.9). London: Pluto Press.

14. Mansfield, R. (2001) How I Became a Video Activist. In T. Harding (ed.) *The Video Activist Handbook* (2nd ed.) (p.13). London: Pluto Press.

15. Ofcom (2015) *Ofcom Broadcast Bulletin*, Issue number 261, 8 September 2014, pp.52–70. Available at http://stakeholders.ofcom.org.uk/binaries/enforcement/broadcast-bulletins/obb2601/obb261.pdf, accessed on 25 April 2015.

UNDERCOVER TALES

True Stories of DIY Filming

Vanessa Evans is a seemingly ordinary woman whose experience using hidden cameras I know particularly well, because she worked with me on a *Panorama* film based partly on the secret footage she recorded.

She is not a journalist; she lives in Croydon, works long hours as a childminder, has a young child herself and, on top of that, always used to look after her grandmother. To her it was just natural; she was always her grandmother's main carer.

The grandmother, Yvonne Grant, was also a Croydon lady. A hard-working woman, she had laboured as a seamstress and finally was head of dressmaking in a Croydon department store for most of her life. She lived her whole life in South London. She was part of the community.

Eventually, though, Yvonne needed more care than Vanessa could provide. There were particular things, like needing help with getting to the toilet, which were difficult for Yvonne unless she had care right there with her. Until the end, Yvonne 'maintained her dignity' as she saw it: going to the toilet and not using an incontinence pad was vitally important to her.

The care home Yvonne moved into was the best that the council was willing to fund, Vanessa says. A 61-bed institution, the home was on the corner of a roundabout but otherwise was surrounded by residential housing. However, from the off, Vanessa was not happy with what she saw. She remembers that Yvonne:

> ...was constantly waiting and asking for the toilet. Every time I went in she'd say, 'Oh, I've been asking, I desperately need the toilet, no one will take me.' I would hear her calling them, and she'd be told, 'in a minute', or 'after you've eaten', or 'you can't go now because there's no staff, one's on break'. A lot of the time she'd be waiting, sometimes up to an hour, even with me going and asking. We had to wait.

It was not just worries about the toilet – as upsetting and indeed potentially painful as that could be for her grandmother. Vanessa says that there were also worrying bruises. Vanessa also had concerns about the attitude of some staff. She made complaints about what she saw but wasn't satisfied with the response.

'I'd go in there and she'd start crying and she'd say, "I just don't want to be here anymore." I knew that something wasn't right, but exactly what I didn't know, or I didn't know until I put in the camera,' Vanessa told us for the film we broadcast on *Panorama*.

Whether to put in a secret camera was a debate, as it was a challenge. Was it necessary to use hidden cameras? Was it proportionate? Was there another way that the problems could be resolved?

A while later, I asked Vanessa to reflect back on her experience – to think about what went well and what she would do differently if she had her time again. What she told me was very interesting for people doing their own filming in future, because it epitomises the fine balance involved with these considerations.

Vanessa told me that she would get a camera in that room sooner, but that she would have gathered better evidence before she began.

She wishes she had taken photographs, demanded copies of paperwork, care plans and body maps, and that she had kept better notes so she could better prove what her worries were initially, before she used a hidden camera. She also would have pushed harder for change – she wishes she had not been fobbed off (as she saw it) with what she says were pat answers from care workers, like 'Oh your nan is just confused.' She thinks that in future other families need to listen to their own gut feelings more, if they know something is wrong.

Vanessa only did her secret filming after she concluded all other options had failed. She is a model of good practice, really. The fact that she wishes that she had pushed harder in all ways and all directions is a testament to the same truth that this book is aiming at: we can all do secret filming better.

It is good, though sad, that Vanessa felt she did have to use secret cameras.

Her hidden camera captured one harrowing hour on a Saturday night when her grandmother became increasingly desperate for the toilet after a cup of tea. She needed the toilet. She called out asking for help – she could not get there on her own. She waited, and then she cried out again. And again. No one came. Despite being just opposite the nursing station, it took more than an hour for a member of staff to come into her room. On that Saturday night, Vanessa's grandmother called out 'nurse' 321 times, pleaded for the toilet 45 times and banged her cup on 26 occasions before anyone checked on her – and even then, after she had been checked on, Yvonne was still left waiting longer for the toilet, becoming increasingly and clearly desperate.

I really want the toilet.

Yvonne Grant pleading with a care worker
Source: BBC (2014) Panorama: Behind Closed Doors: Elderly
Care Exposed. BBC1, 30 April (21:00 hrs). Copyright © BBC

Vanessa told us:

> It was heartbreaking, absolutely heartbreaking. My nan should have been getting good care from the day she went in there; it's what everyone should be getting. It shouldn't take them to be worried that I might have a camera in there – 'so we'd better go in there and give good care just in case' – that they never know if the camera's going to be there or not. It shouldn't take that.

The owners of the care home, HC-One, told BBC *Panorama* when that film was broadcast:

> The failings in the care of Mrs Yvonne Grant, and the behaviour of a number of members of staff at the home at that time, were completely unacceptable. The level of care Mrs Grant received at Oban House during that period was simply not good enough and did not meet the standards that HC-One, as a responsible provider, expects of all our staff at all our homes. We deeply regret these failings and we apologised to Mrs Grant and her family members as soon as they came to light.

By the time our film broadcast – some time after Vanessa's secret recording – the care home met all necessary standards, and HC-One said that they took 'a great many steps to improve the standards of care', including working 'with the new management and staff at the home, and with the active involvement of residents and relatives to implement a significant number of improvements'.

Other people around the world using hidden cameras have not always handled their discoveries as well as Vanessa did. One case that I have only read about, where I do not know personally the people involved, really illustrates the dangers involved when people do their own secret filming.

In that case, in 2014 in Uganda, a non-governmental organisation's employee, Eric Kamanzi, found bruises on his 18-month-old daughter. Rather than confronting his 22-year-old maid, Jolly Tumuhirwe, he installed hidden cameras.

What he filmed was shocking, but what happened after that illustrates how much better prepared everyone needs to be for people doing their own secret filming.

The video footage captured by Kamanzi was broadcast on websites around the world. It shows the maid beating and kicking his daughter.[1] From prison, Tumuhirwe said that she was sorry, that Kamanzi's wife sometimes slaps the child and that she was more angry than normal that day because her father was ill.[2]

Kamanzi allegedly beat Tumuhirwe 'to a pulp' when he saw the footage. Given the severity of the assault on his daughter, some parents will excuse him, but that is not how justice should be administered and, worse, it meant that, of course, he was the one who was arrested, at least initially. Ugandan police were then presented with his covert footage. The police now had to decide what to do with such a mixed set of assaults – one on a child and one on the maid – before finally deciding to pursue Tumuhirwe, not Kamanzi.

People using covert recorders need to think very carefully about how they will react – and hopefully how they will control themselves – if they do film bad events, to prevent themselves from doing wrong and becoming the person who gets arrested. Hopefully, in future, people in such a position will prepare themselves better for the issues that they may have to face.

NOTES

1. Gillman, O. (2014) 'Ugandan maid who sparked outrage when she was filmed stomping on toddler is jailed for four years.' Available at www.dailymail.co.uk/news/article-2874502/Ugandan-maid-sparked-outrage-filmed-stomping-toddler-jailed-four-years.html#ixzz3NOD7xt2z, accessed on 25 July 2015.

2. Nehanda Radio (2014) 'Uganda "monster maid" explains why she beat up child.' Available at http://nehandaradio.com/2014/11/29/uganda-monster-maid-explains-beat-child/#sthash.rbLXAArq.dpuf, accessed on 25 July 2015.

Chapter 2

'PROPER' SECRET CAMERAS

Secret Filming Using a Covert Camera

A search for 'spy camera' on an Internet search engine turns up over 5 million results, including everything from 'proper' secret cameras to much simpler devices. Other searches will turn up a range of covert devices, such as the voice-activated dictating machine that a good friend of mine purchased online.

This friend was worried about his wife's behaviour. He was away for work a lot and feared 'the worst'. Not too long ago, a voice-activated audio recorder would have belonged to the world of James Bond, but now it did not cost the earth to get one and leave it in the drawer of the desk in his study.

My friend's wife was cheating on him. The audio he recorded left no doubt.

That friend managed to use secret recording equipment successfully, but too often members of the public using covert recording equipment do not manage so well. I have seen too many mistakes – sometimes people have been caught out as a result.

Citizen journalists, social campaigners and concerned families do not have to be 'unprofessional'. Most 'civilian' would-be undercover film-makers are still getting it wrong. With just a little bit of knowledge, people doing secret filming can avoid the sort of mistakes that every greenhorn (just like I was once) has made.

Basic mistakes are easy to make. For example, people frequently do point the camera in the wrong direction, leave it recording too briefly, lose some of the original footage and so forth. These things can be avoided if people follow a few simple rules.

This chapter (and indeed this book) is focused on the types of secret cameras members of the public use. The cameras ordinary people buy tend to be ones hidden inside objects that can be plugged in and left to record for many hours (not unlike a CCTV camera, but hidden). There are other types of secret cameras that are less appropriate for 'civilians' and are therefore not discussed in any detail in this book. For example, one can get hidden cameras that are secreted in bags or even worn inside clothing. Those cameras are often called 'bodyworn-' or 'bag-' cameras. It is particularly important that those hidden cameras are used only with support and after proper training; it is much easier to be discovered when using them, even if one just stands differently or switches them on and off too obviously. Being caught with any type of hidden recorder can lead to angry reactions and even harm. If in doubt, anyone using hidden cameras should stop filming or seek advice and help, from the authorities if necessary. Also, there are additional constraints with 'bodyworn-' and 'bag-' cameras (particularly the duration and size of batteries).

THE KNOWLEDGE: HOW TO FILM WITH A 'PROPER' SECRET CAMERA

Rule 1: Shop around before buying; not all cameras are worth purchasing

The main difference between 'proper' covert filming equipment and any other camera is actually the fact that the recorder and the lens are physically separated from each other. The lens is tiny and at the end of a cable which runs to the recorder.

That separation of the lens from the recorder is critical. It is what allows the lens to be hidden in almost anything, with a recorder some distance away. For example, the actual recorder can be at the back of a machine, in a pocket or really anywhere. The lens can be disguised in any tiny hole, button, tear or design.

Obviously, using 'proper' secret cameras requires more active engagement and forethought than using a mobile or cellular phone to film something (as in Chapter 1). No one already has a secret camera with them. Someone has to go out and buy the thing.

Right now, when I switch on my laptop and open up an Internet browser, I can immediately access any number of covert cameras online, or I can cycle into Central London to a specialist 'spy shop', or a number of electronics stores in pretty much any town, and find miniature lenses and recorders.

The fact that cameras are widely available does not mean that they are all worth buying. There is a lot of rubbish being sold out there. One has to be able to distinguish what they need. For example, my father purchased a covert camera on the Internet in order to watch his dog. He wanted to know what little Sandy, a copper-coloured cocker spaniel, was doing during the night, while he slept. 'The damn camera didn't work,' he told me.

There is a huge variation in the cost of secret recording devices available on the Internet. One person I know who recorded extraordinary secret footage spent just £20 on the camera they used, but most of the people I have worked with needed to spend in the region of £200 (over US$300).

I appreciate that is a big investment, but if you look at my father's experience, you can see why it's worth it.

It can seem a little bewildering.

The trick is to not be daunted. Secret filming can be very simple. A number of television investigations and lots of surveillance filming have been done with a camera stuffed into the bottom of a bag which has a hole cut in the corner. That hole needs to be disguised – for example, with the sort of neutral-density filter (see-through plastic, basically) available from proper photographic or camera stores. I have built several basic 'bag cameras' over the years that were no more complicated than that.

Even the sort of hidden camera that one would buy over the Internet is at root also quite basic. A secret camera is really just a lens, a cable and a recorder which have been hidden in anything. It is possible to make perfectly good systems from very basic kit: handheld video players and recorders (that look a bit like a Game Boy or a TomTom) can become a secret camera if they are hooked up to a small remote camera lens and hidden in something.

The only question is how well they are hidden, and whether anyone will notice.

I am not suggesting that citizen journalists go back to basics and build their own cameras, unless one is very technically savvy, but I hope this illustrates how little is involved in demystifying the business of secret recording.

Rule 2: Do not just consider what is on the box, think about what is in the box

PART 1: MEMORY CARDS VS HARD DRIVES

It is easy to obsess about the outside of a secret camera (the disguise or hide that goes over the top). Don't get me wrong, that is important and I will discuss it below, but how the camera works *inside* can be just as important. People who have done their own secret filming often did not realise the implications of different possible configurations. Two key choices are whether to use memory cards (i.e. the same type of thumbnail-sized black computer chip that is in most mobile or cellular phones) or hard drives (i.e. a built-in memory unit), and whether to use a voice- or motion-activated recorder.

First, then, how do you decide whether to use a camera that has a hard drive or one that uses memory cards?

Deep inside a secret camera there is either a slot into which memory cards are inserted, or else a hard drive. Everything is a trade-off. There are pluses and minuses to both configurations.

In the case of a memory card, when it is full, it can be popped out and put in a card reader (widely available at electronic or computer stores), and then downloaded and backed up on to a computer. This is easy enough, as long as one already knows how to use a memory card.

The alternative is a hard-wired hard drive built into the machine. No cards come in or out. Instead, there is a bigger internal memory that is buried inside the bowels of the machine. In order to get anything off the recorder, one has to plug the whole recorder into their computer to retrieve the footage.

The right decision depends on the answers to a few questions:

» *How easy will it be to get the whole secret camera in and out of its setting?*

The reason this matters is that anyone using a hard drive will only be able to recover their footage when they get the whole thing out, and can only start filming again when they get the whole thing back in (unless they buy two at the outset and swap the recorders every time they go in and out of a location). The main advantage that removable memory cards have is that one does not have to smuggle the whole camera in and out of wherever they are filming every time they need to download the footage.

» *How confident am I about using, removing and backing up memory cards?*

Hard drives are more solid and so tend to be a safer way to handle footage.[3] Unless a hard drive is physically broken into pieces or dropped in water, it will usually hold all the data safely until a recorder is plugged into a computer. Little memory cards are riskier. One scratch, one bend and everything is lost. If the point of contact is damaged, then a computer won't be able to read the card and so the footage will be as good as lost, unless it is taken to specialists in data recovery, which is expensive. It is not often that people lose data because they bend or scratch memory cards, but it does happen.

This is a real-life decision which has an actual impact, not a theoretical technical difference. Vanessa Evans, who filmed her grandmother's mistreatment in a care home (see 'Undercover Tales' at the end of Chapter 1), bought a camera that relied on a hard drive.

Vanessa had to take the whole secret camera back to her home to download the footage. That meant she had to smuggle the camera in, smuggle it back out, download the footage and then bring back the camera – now empty and ready to record – and set it rolling again.

She now wishes she had bought *two* cameras so she could have set one recording while the other was downloading. 'Because I only had one, I could only record at night, so I don't know what was going on during the day,' she recalled.

The bottom line is that there are no 'good' or 'bad' configurations, just different ways of doing things that suit different settings better or worse. It is worth thinking carefully about the implications of the different types of secret camera that are available.

PART 2: MOTION ACTIVATION; THE MEMORY FILLING UP; AND LIGHT AND SOUND

A number of the 'proper' secret cameras being sold on the Internet have motion-activated options. Two of the families I worked with used that setting. Their thinking was that they would use up less space on their memory card or hard drive if they only filmed when something was happening. The same was true for my friend (mentioned previously) who recorded his wife's infidelity using a voice-activated audio recorder.

Motion activation sounds great in theory but is rife with problems in practice. The first problem is that it means the footage always misses the beginning of any encounter. If the lens has to identify movement before it kicks into gear, then it will never catch the nature and tone of the greeting. Beginnings can be important. Did someone come crashing in looking for trouble, or were they provoked from the off?

Second, motion-activated cameras (or voice-activated recorders) are in my experience intrinsically unstable. They inexplicably and unavoidably misbehave. Whatever the manufacturers of such systems say, the footage I have seen has errors; for example, despite motion continuing, the camera has switched itself off. All secret filming is at risk of mechanical frailty – machines can always cut out or have picture or sound drop out – but building in another possibility for switching on and off increases the risk.

I would strongly advise against cameras that switch themselves on and off. My experience suggests that everyone should try (if it is possible and feasible) to just leave the camera recording or switch it on and off themselves when needed (again, if that is possible).

Before buying a secret camera, one needs to consider all those advantages and disadvantages. Depending on the situation they are filming, one configuration or another might be best. It will usually come down to how safe and easy it is to get the camera in and out of wherever filming is taking place.

There are three other technical things that I would advise people to consider or check before buying a secret camera, none of which citizen journalists seem to realise or consider at the moment.

The first thing can be a bit of a shock. In a number of cameras I have seen people use, once the memory card or hard drive is full, it starts recording back over the beginning of whatever was already recorded. That can erase important evidence. Anyone buying a recorder should check before they get a nasty surprise.

The two other important technical differences between the types of secret camera on the market at the moment are light and sound. (There are also options regarding lenses and microphones.)

Depending on how a camera is configured, it can respond better or worse to low-light conditions. If someone needs to film in the dark, then it is important before buying to ask any supplier how well their different lenses or cameras adapt to low light.

For example, black-and-white lenses operate better in the dark, but I think that most citizen journalists or social activists are unlikely to want to learn about the different technical options available. The more important thing is to consider the setting where the camera will be used and then discuss that with the manufacturer or salesman.

Depending on the location of filming, one should also ask what microphone to use.

Between sound and picture, it is easy to focus more on the picture. No one would deny pictures are pretty important. Particularly if a camera will need to operate in low light, it is important that it is able to adjust to the dark. However, it is usually the sound that actually matters most to producing evidence that has the greatest impact.

One family I worked with recorded evidence that led to a care worker being convicted for manhandling their relative. However, the critical thing in terms of people being convicted was that the jury could hear what the workers were saying. It proved their ill intent and their frame of mind. When the footage was played back, the disgust in their tone of voice was palpable. That sound was what put the nature of their movements and their motivation beyond dispute.

The sound is often what makes it possible to really understand what is going on. Without it, defendants in a court case or people facing accusations in the media can invent any number of excuses based on what they claim they were saying. That is not just hypothetical – in one court case I followed, the police managed to lose the sound and a defendant was able to paint an entirely different picture of what had gone on. Thankfully, the jury didn't buy it. The man was still convicted.

There are different types of microphones. One type records all ambient noise in almost all directions. That can be good if someone cannot know in which direction the most important events will take place, but that will mean they are going to pick up a lot more 'interference' and 'noises off'. There are also directional microphones that record only in an arc directly in front of them.

Again, though, as with different types of lenses, I do not expect most people buying a camera off the Internet to want too much detail about the microphones on the market. The bottom line is that just as with asking what happens when the card or recorder is full, it is also worth asking questions about the sound, even if only to be clear where the microphone is to be hidden.

That will allow one to consider whether it would be muffled by anything, or how the device could be positioned so that the microphone is least blocked.

A little preparation, a little care and a little attention to detail can go a long way.

Rule 3: Don't get caught (what is on the outside matters, too)

Even though 'proper' hidden cameras are tucked away in an outer skin or hide, they can still be discovered, and when people realise they are being filmed, they often react badly. It is not pleasant, and it can be dangerous.

A person only gets one chance to sneak up on the 'bad guy'. One who gets it wrong could be discovered. That is not a theoretical concern. I know examples where it has happened. The professional undercover journalists I know who were discovered wearing cameras hidden in their clothing were literally caught in the act either of putting their camera away or else a wire fell out. A wire hanging down or a recorder held out is pretty incontrovertible. Once busted, they had to run for it.

Citizen journalists, worried activists and others are less and less (in my experience) wearing their cameras hidden in their clothing – they are leaving them in a room and collecting the footage later. That creates a different dilemma. How does one know if their camera has been unmasked? Could they be walking into a trap? It could be dangerous.

One woman contacted me and a colleague about problems with the treatment of her husband in a care home. The colleague and I begged her to gather more evidence before using a hidden camera. She was not prepared to wait. She was going to get her own camera quickly and get it in there.

We explained that she had to think carefully, that given *we* could not secretly film, we would not encourage her to do it. We explained that if she did press ahead, she needed to think about what sort of objects were already in place in the room. We told her to replace like with like, so that no one would notice. But she did not listen to any of our advice. She bought a camera that looked nothing like anything already in the room and put it in. The result was pretty predictable. On the first night she put it in the care home, care workers turned it face down. The second night it was covered with a cloth. The third night a good care worker, who was out of the loop and not one of the clique the woman was worried about, was filmed. This care worker wasn't great, but she also wasn't setting out to do anything wrong.

I would not be surprised if in the end the hidden camera was 'accidentally' smashed.

And even that would not be the worst possible outcome. The scariest possibility is that someone could realise they were being filmed and be so irritated that they took some kind of revenge, either on the woman who hid the camera or, even worse, on her vulnerable relative. The danger of secretly filming badly, of getting it wrong, is potentially grave.

Ideally, one should always be looking to replace something that does not have a camera in it with something that does have a camera in it: a light for a light, a TV for a TV, a DVD recorder for a DVD recorder, an air freshener for an air freshener.[4] Like for like.

The best hide will depend entirely on the circumstances where one is intending to film.

Sadly, for people doing secret filming in future, the truth is that the dangers are getting worse. The targets of secret filming are getting better at recognising it and catching people before they record anything. As the general public gets more aware and therefore more able to use hidden cameras, the people they would wish to film are getting more savvy. The targets of possible filming now look for strange new objects and try to see any changes that might indicate a camera.

As secret filming becomes more common, it also becomes more dangerous. Start slowly and go carefully.

Rule 4: Point the camera straight at what needs to be recorded

After one has picked a hide, they have to face the scariest, most hair-raising part of the job: one has to smuggle the camera in somewhere and hope that no one will notice.

People often make terrible mistakes placing their cameras badly as a result of the fear and the need for speed. All the expense and effort to select and hide a camera is meaningless if people carrying out secret filming don't make sure to carefully point the camera squarely at the target – at wherever the wrongdoing they are concerned about is most likely to occur and just wide enough to see the context; what is going on around. Striking this balance in order to film a good 'frame' can be difficult for people who have not used secret cameras before, because most hidden cameras do not have viewing screens. Usually that means that someone cannot check what they are doing when they start to record. As a result, there are only three ways to get it right: (1) blind luck; (2) practising again and again before installation, to learn the angle at which the lens films; and (3) filming in circumstances where it is both easy and safe to adjust the camera repeatedly, unobserved, after reviewing the secretly recorded footage.

Mandy Mugford is another member of the public, like Vanessa Evans, who filmed the care that her mother,

Margaret Heslop, received in a nursing home. Mandy had thought carefully about which secret camera she would purchase and how she would ensure it was not discovered. She found a clock that was similar to one already in the room. She explained:

> I didn't buy a cheap one because I was fearful of it not taping as well as it should. That's not to say it wouldn't, but I wanted to make sure that whatever footage I got was worthy of seeing, so that's why I went for this one. The clock we had on the wall before was quite big. So that's why I went with that one.

Even though she bought it ready-made, Mandy still decided that she needed to do more work to ensure that the camera would not be discovered. She told us, 'You can see the stickers I put on. I made sure that I covered up the lights and so forth on the camera.'

That sort of extra effort may be why her camera was not discovered.

Mandy put the secret camera in her mother's room successfully, and it was pointing at her mother (which is a lot better than some people manage); however, she deliberately decided to put the camera so it only filmed her mother's top half, to try to preserve her mother's dignity, in the actual rushes (i.e. the unedited film images).

I respect that decision. Maybe she was right, but as a general principle I would strongly advise other people never to do that. It is effectively editing in the camera.

This is one of the most vexed – and potentially risky – legal and ethical areas of covert recording and hidden cameras. Particularly if one is filming vulnerable people, even a first-degree relative has to carefully consider recording, handling and storing any footage that includes nudity. It is the most extreme invasion of privacy.

In a later chapter I generally advise employees (some of whom are whistle-blowers) against recording or storing images that compromise a vulnerable person's dignity – or at least suggest they seek advice before doing so (see 'Undercover Tales' at the end of Chapter 5). However, other people using hidden cameras are often the relative of a potential victim or actually the potential victim themselves. If they have really pursued all other avenues of complaint, have sought legal advice where necessary and are pursuing evidence of genuinely illegal or serious antisocial behaviour, then, depending on the circumstances, the primary concern is likely to no longer be privacy; it is gathering clear enough evidence to prevent the wrongdoing continuing in future.

If a member of the public buys a camera because they are worried about how someone is being treated, it's important to point the camera so that as much of the person as possible is in the frame; otherwise, the person filming will have gone to all this effort and could find (bluntly) that the activity they need evidence about happened at the part of the person they are not filming.

Anyone doing any covert filming has to trust that it is possible to preserve someone's dignity later. If the footage ends up with a film-maker like me, then we have a range of options available once we take the footage into edit. We have sometimes indelibly obscured (i.e. blurred) worrying elements or cropped images to preserve dignity even in the rushes – so that someone can have confidence that any nudity or other issue is permanently resolved.

Even average computer-literate members of the public can work out how to resolve the most basic issues themselves. Increasingly, teenagers are cutting their own mini-videos using basic desktop editing programmes. An Internet search will identify different free video-editing software options, all of which have basic blurring or even 'spray can' tools.

It is not possible to judge every situation, and there may be circumstances where this is not appropriate; however, nudity or truly extreme invasion of privacy can be protected later, but it is impossible to 'put evidence back' in that which was not filmed in the first place.

These decisions are difficult, but if a situation deserves to be covertly filmed at all, then it is worth filming the whole situation. If the evidence justifies invading someone's privacy, then it is worth making sure that professionals relying on that evidence can really see what is happening. One of my bosses, Frank Simmonds, puts it nicely when he says, 'You can't be half pregnant.' If someone does have to secretly film in order to stop something, then I would argue it is usually better to secretly film as completely as possible.

Rule 5: Practice makes perfect (or at least read the instructions)

Sometimes doing good secret filming means going to extreme lengths. For example, I train the undercover operatives who work for me, and who usually wear cameras hidden in their clothes, not to breathe during critical moments of evidence gathering. Literally, they are expected to hold still and stop breathing until whatever is important has finished. And it works. The result is that I can see and hear better what is happening, because the camera is not rising and falling with each breath.

Vanessa Evans has some straightforward advice for anyone following in her footsteps and using hidden cameras:

I wish I had known how to use it properly. I just bought one off the Internet, then scoured the supermarkets for a dummy [an object that looked exactly the same but without a camera in it], just scanned the instructions, pushed this button and hoped for the best. I really just spent a lot of money and prayed.

A bit of time, even a couple hours really reading the instruction manual, even asking questions of the supplier and ideally doing a test-run at home, can save a lot of frustration later. The best way to ensure a secret camera works is to test, test and then test again – before installing it.

Rule 6: Handle the kit very, very (very) carefully

There is a final technical lesson for anyone doing secret filming that I have held back until the end, mainly because it is a little embarrassing. This rule could have been called 'why things go wrong'.

When I was starting out, there were a number of times the camera lost its picture or didn't have sound on it – and often it was my fault. I later reviewed the rushes on those days things went wrong and would be furious. I would curse and shout about the camera, saying it had let me down. The truth, I now realise, is that I was at fault; I had let down the camera.

Almost every time the camera 'failed', what had actually happened was that I had either stretched a cable too far, twisted a connection, put a battery in the wrong way or not quite made a good connection with the tape or memory card.

Every single connection, every cable, every plug, every part of a secret camera needs to be handled gently and cautiously, carefully and thoughtfully. If one has risked everything to smuggle a recording device into a critical situation, don't they owe it to their own efforts to make sure they don't blow it by breaking the camera?

Go gently and carefully.

NOTES

1. BBC (2012) *Panorama: Undercover: Elderly Care.* BBC1, 23 April. Also see BBC (2012) 'Regulator criticised after woman assaulted in care home.' Available at www.bbc.co.uk/news/health-17777113, accessed on 22 March 2015; and Daily Mail Reporter (2012) 'Nurse filmed assaulting dementia patient, 80, on daughter's secret camera.' Available at www.dailymail.co.uk/news/article-2129417/Care-home-worker-caught-slapping-helpless-Alzheimers-victim-bed-jailed-18-months, accessed on 25 April 2015.

2. At the time we broadcast that film, the owners of the care home told the BBC that the assault was an isolated incident, that they were 'committed to working closely with all families and residents' and that they receive positive feedback on their care, which is subject to 'continual improvement'.

3. Readers who want more detail should speak to covert camera salespeople or an engineer, but I should explain that I have written 'tend to be a safer way' because there are different types of hard drives used in secret recorders, some of which, for example, have moving parts inside that over time are more likely to wear down and stop working. In other words, secretly recorded video footage actually *can* be less 'safe' on a hard drive than if it was stored on a removable memory card, but that is just in certain specific circumstances – for example, if a hard drive is used (not new) and has those moving parts. That will not be an issue if someone is only using a brand-new hidden camera for a short period of time. One can learn more about the differences between types of hard drives if one searches the library or the Internet for terms such as 'hard disk drive' or 'HDD', 'solid state drive' or 'SSD' and 'solid state hybrid drive' or 'SSHD'.

4. Astute readers and media professionals who already work with hidden cameras will note that this chapter has not discussed battery power – the main limiting factor on cameras journalists use, hidden on their body – and that all the examples listed here can be plugged in. All the people I have worked with who did their own secret filming used cameras hidden in electrical equipment that did not have to rely on battery power. If someone does choose to use a secret camera which is not plugged in, then they will be constrained by their battery.

UNDERCOVER TALES

Eek! Nearly Being Discovered

Ideally, no one else would have to learn how easily secret cameras can be discovered the way I did.

This was in 2003. I was still wearing secret cameras hidden on my clothes and going undercover. The technology was so bulky back then that it seems miraculous we weren't *all* caught, all the time. We had to use great big clunky cameras, with mini-video cassette tapes and thick cables, all strapped to our bodies in elasticated belts tucked around our chests and under our armpits.

I was working alongside a young man whom I'll call Paul, going door to door between different houses. I was undercover, again, making a film about a gas and electricity company whose agents were breaking rules, effectively mis-selling contracts and tricking customers.

This salesman, Paul, had no idea that I was wearing a camera hidden in my tie.

I had been warned that ties are dangerous, easy to spot, but I had chosen one anyway.

Paul had been taught by his bosses to get people to change providers to his company without them even realising what had happened. For example, I saw him repeatedly jot down the numbers he needed from their current gas bill and then swap them on to his company, without them even knowing he had done it. They thought he was just checking their bill.

He talked really fast:

'Those are the six sections of the sales pitch; you run it just like that. That's all it is.'

Again and again, running through what they say to people: 'Hi, I'm here to see if you qualify for a rebate. Can you get your latest gas bill?' … 'Right, you do qualify. Can you just sign here and here?'

He kept going over and over it with me constantly as we walked suburban streets, up one street and down the next, knocking on doors, and between each running through his patter, his pitch – first with me to teach me, then for real with a customer, and then as soon as we were out the door continuing on with me, taking me through my training. It was incessant. He was almost cult-like in his recitation of the sales pitch and his search for money.

We were both in cheap, scratchy, ill-fitting suits, young men with shoulder bags strapped across our chests; kids pretending to be adults, trying to work the world out. Paul had really been sucked into a belief in a possible future. He told me again and again that if he carried on long enough, he might be able to be a middle manager and set up his own sales group. This short, focused, intense young man was ignoring – or at least not saying out loud – that 'carrying on long enough' actually meant *cheating enough people.*

Then all at once he stopped talking, mid-sentence.

I can remember it in slow motion, but it must have happened in a second.

'So then you go on to the confirmation…' He stops. His hand flashes out, without warning, like a snake jumping out of its basket, flying at my Achilles' heel: the hidden camera.

His fist clenches my tie, its camera hidden in a little bulge. Mid-sentence, halfway through explaining how his company cheats innocent people, he's holding my camera.

'What's that in your tie?' he demands.

No warning. No way to avoid it. I'm pulling away, pulling my tie out of Paul's hand. His eyes are burning into it. There's a pause that feels like minutes but in reality is only moments.

'Hey, man, that's my chest,' I finally say.

'No – there's something in your tie.'

'It's just a cheap tie.'

Turning away from him, facing the building across the way, I am desperate, just babbling.

There is no way out, now, surely. I've been caught, right?

I have no plan except to try to get back across the housing estate to the car, calling in my (then) producer, Andrew Head, who's sitting somewhere up the road.

Then I was saved. By chance. By dumb luck.

Immediately before Paul had grabbed my tie, he had rung another house's doorbell. I'd totally forgotten. Just as I was getting ready to run away, the door of that house opened, disgorging another member of the public, someone else who Paul could try to make money off.

'Can I help you?'

The training Paul had been given kicked in and he ran straight into his sales pitch.

By the time the dust settled on his forms and the new customer's numbers, Paul had thankfully forgotten all about my 'cheap tie'. He had caught me, and yet I had gotten away with it.[1]

I know members of the public and undercover journalists who have been caught using secret cameras. In almost every case there was either arrogance like mine – not listening to advice, basically – or sloppiness at the root of the problem. Trying to film someone without them realising is inherently risky and requires always being on guard, focused and ever so slightly humble.

One cannot be too careful – and will always need a fair helping of luck.

NOTES

1. BBC (2003) *Inside Out: Rogue energy salespeople.* BBC1, 13 October 2003 [no longer available online]. See BBC (2013) 'Rogue energy salespeople.' Available at www.bbc.co.uk/insideout/south/series4/rogue_salesman.shtml, accessed on 26 July 2015.

Chapter 3

USING A PHONE CAMERA SECRETLY

Covert Recording Using a Mobile or Cellular Telephone

Russell Sharp was both an undercover reporter for the BBC and an infantry soldier when he joined the British Army in order to investigate the bullying of young recruits by the men paid to train them. Russell wrote the following at the time a film was broadcast based on his experiences:

> My life became waking up at 5.30 or 6am, impeccable ironing, constant cleaning, tight timings and lots of marching. At least that's what I was doing when I wasn't getting army fit. My back, legs and arms have never hurt as much as the times we had to run with a huge log over hills for a couple of miles.[1]

Russell Sharp, Undercover Soldier
Source: Copyright © BBC 2008

Russell exposed mistreatment of young men who had joined the army to fight for their country. These young recruits were ready to die for their country, if necessary, but they had not joined up in order to be randomly beaten in the toilet by a trainer. Some of the new recruits around Russell were just 16 years old and straight off some of the poorest housing estates in Britain.

Young men who join the army need to be hardened if they are to face the rigours of military life. Non-commissioned officers (NCOs) have to toughen them up and enforce discipline. There is no other option given what they are required to do. NCOs could shout at the young recruits, make them run as far as needed or make them do as many sit ups as required; however, some went much further than they needed and much further than did any good. Russell wrote:

In my platoon I saw two corporals lose their temper and break the rules, punching recruits or grabbing them by the neck and throwing them to the ground. One recruit was even urinated on by a corporal as he lay prone waiting to fire his loaded rifle... On the live firing range I saw a corporal smash two recruits' helmets together and kick one of them... I also got the chance to speak to some of the lads in the other platoon. One told me he was kicked and punched by a corporal. Another describes being punched to the ground by one of his instructors. He says his hand was injured as he tried to defend himself from further blows.

It was unprofessional and unnecessary, Russell felt. It didn't scare recruits any worse than the 'beasting' – the massive quantities of heavy-duty exercise that could be meted out. The violence was extracurricular, a few individuals exploiting their position, breaking the rule and the law.

At the time we broadcast that film, the Ministry of Defence told the BBC it had already been in the process of investigating several of the cases brought to them by the BBC documentary team:

...where allegations were new, we immediately launched further investigations.

We are, however, unable to comment on the details of specific cases so that we do not prejudice ongoing legal processes. Bullying is absolutely unacceptable and fundamentally at odds with the Army's core values. All soldiers are made aware that if they are a victim of bullying then they can complain either through their chain of command or to the independent Service Complaints Commissioner. We keep the standards of training across all Army facilities under constant review to ensure that the core values are being observed, and our training establishments are also the subject of continuous scrutiny by external, independent authorities.

Russell put himself at huge personal risk in order to smuggle a series of 'proper' professional secret cameras into the British Army, but despite having those professionally built cameras, the most compelling evidence was recorded using Russell's telephone. Cutting the record light inside his phone[2] so it did not light up was probably the most important thing that we did.

That evidence led to four convictions. One NCO pleaded guilty to a charge of battery. A second NCO pleaded guilty to two charges: ill treatment of a soldier and conduct prejudicial to good order and military discipline. Two other army trainers were found guilty of one or more charges of ill treatment. Russell recalled:

My mobile phone became the most practical tool for recording.

Those were tough conditions. There were regular checks by non-commissioned officers and high security. Plus we spent most of our day exposed to the elements. The high unpredictability meant the real secret cameras were often impracticable. Everyone always had a mobile phone. It was always available.

That experience of the versatility and potential for phones to carry out covert recording has been replicated on a smaller scale by innumerable citizen journalists across the world. The difference between phone cameras and more professional or 'proper' secret cameras is actually mainly presentational. The phone in everyone's pocket right now includes a microphone, a lens and can record on to a memory card or its own internal memory.

That is all that is needed.

PEOPLE USING MOBILE OR CELLULAR TELEPHONES NEED TO BE PREPARED

Even though a lot of secret filming is now being conducted with mobile or cellular telephones, most of it is not being done well and is not being done as safely as it could be. Anyone who thinks that they might need to use their phone as a recording device should take whatever time they can spare, even if it's just ten minutes, to think through what that would involve.

The evidence can be just as strong as filming with 'proper' secret cameras. However, greater forethought is required to improve the quality of the results and also to ensure the safety of everyone involved. Phones are quite simply more dangerous than 'proper' secret cameras; they are by definition less hidden. As a result, the risks involved need to be considered seriously.

Depending on the circumstances, people can put themselves in great danger by using a mobile or cellular phone to record misbehaviour or mistreatment. I have seen examples in the past that put people in genuine danger. For example, one single mother who used to live in Essex was abused by her violent and controlling partner. In the end, she fled to a refuge in a new location for her safety and that of her young daughter.

'I have 278 texts he sent during just two weeks,' she told me. Every step she took her phone would beep, with everything from 'I love you' to saying that he was going to hurt her, or insulting their daughter. He would repeatedly hit her when she stepped out of line.

Finally, trying to convince herself to leave him to prove to herself that she was not going crazy, using her mobile phone she filmed him as he was raging and threatening her in the car one day. Unfortunately, she basically just held up the phone and pointed it at him, record light flaring. He saw it and smashed the phone.

She had enraged him further. She had exacerbated the situation and her danger.

There are risks to all secret filming but particularly so when someone uses the camera in their phone, as it is not designed not to be seen, unless someone is very careful about how they use it.

In 2011, BBC *Panorama* made a 30-minute film following the experience of a necessarily anonymous (for legal reasons and her own protection) woman whose ex-boyfriend had stalked her mercilessly. I was not involved with this film, but someone broke into her house (she believes it was him) and definitely repeatedly stood outside her house threatening her and following her. He was finally prosecuted, but only after she recorded the phone calls he made and filmed him through the frosted glass of a door.

It can be scary to wield a mobile or cellular phone as a secret camera. That is true whether someone is faced by police officers doing something wrong or if they collect evidence of anything else. Collecting proof is different from taking family photos. If activists and campaigners know they may need to defend themselves or show what is being done, then they had better not get caught on the hop. They had better be ready.

THE KNOWLEDGE: HOW TO FILM WITH THE CAMERA SECRETED IN A PHONE

I am used to having 'proper' secret cameras hidden in a range of objects. I have been using them for years. So on those occasions I have used my phone as a secret camera, I have felt very exposed. Secretly filming with the camera in a phone basically just involves hoping that whoever you are filming will not notice, or will not think about it.

If you stay calm and remain sensible, then it will usually be fine. One does need a strong nerve, though. It's not easy to switch a phone into record without anyone noticing and point it at something that needs filming.

A major factor in success may be a bit out of the hands of most readers – at least until their next upgrade comes through or someone offers to buy them a new phone. Filming depends a great deal on what mobile or cellular phone one owns. My iPhone puts itself into record almost instantly with two key presses, but other smartphones can be incredibly fiddly to get into video-recording mode.

Russell Sharp, the undercover soldier who relied mainly on his mobile phone, said:

> I was lucky with the phone I had because to get it into record mode all I had to do was flick a button on the front that opened the camera lens and hit an external button to start recording. It meant I could do it all in

my pocket and bring it out recording without having to look at it or mess about in the open.

Russell told me:

> I think this is *so* hard now with smartphones when it's not possible to set it recording in your pocket pressing the screen. It's OK for general use, but something of the scale I did would need consideration of the type of mobile phone used and the ease to which you can set it to record mode in your pocket.

Russell is absolutely right: do not try to use a phone to film secretly unless you can switch it into record mode in your pocket. Practise doing it before you need to use it.

Rule 1: It can be safer to keep the phone in a pocket (recording audio only)

If someone understands the risks involved with pulling out a phone – given everyone knows they have cameras in them – the first question should be: 'Do I need to pull it out?'

A great deal of evidence can be captured with only audio. It still takes a strong nerve to hold a phone so that the microphone can pick up sounds but be hidden enough (not right out on the table, for example, unless that is somehow normal or nonchalant) to not be suspected.

A care worker approached me to tell of an experience. Because her colleague started swearing at an old woman with dementia, calling her a 'stupid bitch,' she switched on the video camera in her mobile phone. 'But because it has a record light, I couldn't take it out of my pocket, so you can only hear as she threw tissues at her,' she told me. It would have been better in this situation to capture images as well as sound, but it might not have been safe. Being better prepared, given her concerns, might have allowed her to safely capture both sound and picture of what was going on.

Rule 2: Do something about the record light and the loud 'bleep'

The most immediate problem if someone does pull their phone out of their pocket aiming to film is that mobile or cellular phones have record lights on them. I understand those lights are there for a good reason – for example, to discourage perverts from recording up women's skirts without the victim realising.[3]

That record light is less useful if someone is seeking to record and thereby prevent antisocial or illegal behaviour. I do not want to encourage anyone to do anything radical to their phones (not least for fear of a flood of complaints about damaged or broken phones). It is possible to outright cut the cable that feeds electricity to the light, but this is not advisable unless one is very good with electrics and mechanics. It does seem to me that a bit of high-strength adhesive putty (called 'black tack' in the UK) or a piece of duct tape could be just as effective, and is a little less likely to damage the phone, but one tries this at one's own risk.

Next, turn the phone's audio off, as a bleep (or in the case of my current phone a whipping sound that I suspect is meant to mimic a camera shutter closing) can give the game away instantly.

Rule 3: Hold very, very still

Once the camera on a mobile or cellular phone is silent, not lit up and recording, then one is still only at first base; that is just the beginning. Even if one is actually filming and does manage to point the phone in the right direction (neither are a given in the face of stressful situations), they will usually still manage to record precious little of any value.

The reason is that most people do not hold absolutely still.

Too often the footage from a phone is blurry and too brief. The solution is pretty self-evident: If someone is using their phone to film something secretly, they need to avoid waving it about. Ideally, someone should brace their filming arm. If it is not convenient or casual enough to lean against a wall or table, one can at least brace their elbow against their side. Russell Sharp told me the following about his time undercover:

> I used to find a comfortable sitting position and use my lap to rest my arms on letting my hand relax, even though it was holding the phone. This helped me look natural and also provided stability for filming. If standing, arms were dropped naturally by my side to again look normal and make the camera as still as possible.

Holding steady sounds easier than it is. The reality is that secret filming is often nerve-wracking, but once one has gone to all that trouble to capture evidence, the least they should do is ensure someone else is able to see it and hear it. The alternative is massively disappointing to everyone involved. I have been lured to meetings with people who claimed they had recorded evidence of terrible things. They may (or may not, I can't say) have *seen* those things, but what they did not do was film them.

It is painful for all concerned to sit through a meeting with someone like me, trying to argue there is 'evidence' of mistreatment or bad behaviour, where all I can see is a blur, where all I can hear is something that should be relegated to a cereal commercial: 'crackle crackle pop pop'.

I remember the sort of angry, hungry look on someone's face as they asked me, 'Are you *blind?*' How could I not see what they had proven? It was 'obvious' what was happening!

The problem is that it wasn't – not to me or anyone else. The person was deluding themselves. They were 'there' the first time, when it actually happened, so they knew what was going on in the footage. To anyone else it looked and sounded a bit like wibble-wobble-wibble-wobble jelly on a plate, not evidence.

Holding still when using a phone has a second corollary benefit: the more one moves around, the more likely someone is to notice the phone and think, *I wonder if I'm being filmed.* I have known professional undercover operatives who have conducted covert interviews right on their mobile phone without anyone even blinking, just because the phone was held still at their side.

The same is true of audio. Even if a mobile phone is just recording audio hidden away in a pocket, like that care worker mentioned above, moving around is still dangerous. It will draw attention to the fact that there is something in that pocket. If it's on, then just leave it, because moving it around will produce a rustling noise. Holding still really is key.

If footage is shaky and wobbly, it provides poor evidence.

RUSSELL SHARP'S ADVICE

Russell did more secret filming using his phone than anyone before or since. He very kindly offered a few additional tips for people filming:

» **Practice.**

'Do a *lot* of practice on what angles you film, how you have to have the phone tilted, so that you don't have to look at the phone to *know* it is pointed clearly at the target.'

» **Don't look at the phone.**

'Do not look at the phone – ever – or move it away if someone else looks at it (as tempting as this is). This will only draw attention to it.'

» **Think about when you pointedly don't have the phone.**

'Once you are done, or you feel you have had your phone out too long, put it quietly away back in your pocket and gesture (a lot) with open hands to leave a subtle but lasting memory with others that you weren't there the whole time with your phone.'

» **Use the phone to film openly, when possible.**

'It is good to joke around filming something with your phone with someone. Hold the phone camera obviously in a position different from normal and openly and awkwardly. This leaves the impression of what you "look like" when you are filming (i.e. when you don't look like this, you can't be filming!).'

> » **Be aware of what or who is behind you.**
> 'People positioned behind you may be able to see the screen. Make sure you have your back away from people, or if surrounded use your hand or body naturally to shield straying eyes).'

Rule 4: Turn the phone on its side

All mobile or cellular phones have the wrong orientation. It is an unfortunate fact now so ingrained in the technology that it is hard to see it changing. All but a couple of phones I have seen are designed to be held such that the camera films in portrait orientation. It would be infinitely better to film evidence in landscape orientation. This is the right way to film:

Not like this:

Everyone using a phone to film anything – whether covert or overt – should start turning their phone on its side. At the moment, no one turns their phone on its side.

As a result, there have been a number of times when people have brought me important evidence which was filmed in the wrong, second orientation.

The reason why it is important to film everything the right way around is no further away than the nearest television or computer. All screens for broadcast or playback have the same (landscape) orientation, not the other (portrait) orientation, as the first illustration. Phones have almost universally been built with cameras at a different orientation to the television and computer screens on which we watch the footage.

Anyone who films anything in portrait orientation will discover when they come to play back or edit the footage that the result is quite poor. Either the already relatively pixelated and low-resolution image is further squeezed down and made smaller with big black gaps at the side, or it is zoomed in so much that the top and bottom have been cut off.

Either way, the impact of the evidence that has been filmed is lessened.

We all need to get used to filming with our mobile or cellular phones turned on their side.

Rule 5: To increase recording duration, get a high-capacity memory card

The length of time that different mobile or cellular telephones will record video before their battery dies varies enormously. Just as some new smartphones seem to die off mid-call and some older phones seem to allow endless phone conversations, the same is true for filming.

It is worth looking at the manufacturer's instructions to check whether or not there are ways to extend the battery duration (for example, it is sometimes possible to switch off applications that otherwise run in the background). The truth, though, is that there is not much someone can do short of getting a new phone.

The thing that can *definitely* be changed is the size of the memory card inside the phone. My wife's phone, for example, has a 500-MB memory card and seems to always be running out of space (i.e. it won't let her take more photos). My phone with a 2-GB memory card never seems to fill up. Regardless of whether someone knows they will use their phone to secretly record anything, it is better to have a high-capacity memory card, just in case.

Rule 6: Only try to record things where the filming adds value to testimony

Members of the public have sent me a lot of audio recordings, which they made secretly, of meetings. I have always listened diligently to each of the recordings but have yet to hear anything that had sufficient evidential value to justify my investigating further.

I do not want to try to judge what people have done or will do in future: it might be possible that really serious antisocial or illegal activity could take place at a meeting – for example, when someone is lying, threatening or mistreating people and then hiding it from the minutes. Also, recordings can be made for note-taking purposes, simply for someone's own records (although it can in some circumstances be better to declare that fact, i.e. to say outright, 'I am recording this meeting for my notes').

People using their mobile or cellular phones to record stuff in future need to realise that it is only worth secretly filming something where the recording adds value. Secretly recording people who are talking openly and making honest notes of what they say can feel like a betrayal of trust. If the accusation proved by recording is essentially 'they have been saying X is black, when actually it's dark-charcoal grey', one should just make their own written notes; it's usually just as good in that kind of circumstance.

Everyone has a recording device in their pocket if they are bold enough and prepared to carefully take out their phone. More covert recording is going on now using the camera in a mobile or cellular telephone than using 'proper' hidden cameras.

NOTES

1. Sharp, R. (2008) 'I did two jobs – reporter and soldier.' Available at http://news.bbc.co.uk/1/hi/uk/7622493.stm, accessed on 24 January 2015.

2. Cutting a record light in a phone is not something the author would advise that people do. It can only be achieved if someone gets plans to the mechanics inside their phone (which are often available online) to identify the relevant electrical pathway and if that person really knows what they are doing.

3. See, for example, Fersch, E. (2006) *Thinking About the Sexually Dangerous: Answers to Frequently Asked Questions with Case Examples* (p.178). New York, NY: iUniverse.

UNDERCOVER TALES

Sneaky Phone Filming

The filming being done by members of the public with a mobile or cellular telephone is obviously not all covert or secret. People do use their phones to film openly and 'bear witness'. For example, the group Netpol encourages people to film the police doing 'stop and search'. They say, 'More and more people are able to film the actions of the police during a stop and search and are choosing to do so.'[1]

However, there is also a lot of phone footage which is truly secret or covert.

Everyone is so used to filming everything (their child, the dog, a fly crawling across the tarmac – anything) that, in the presence of potential injustice, they often do not stop to ask themselves some basic questions about what they have recorded, namely, 'Have I just filmed evidence of wrongdoing?' and 'Did they know I was filming?'

If the answer to the first question is 'yes' and the answer to the second question is 'no', the filming was probably covert. What defines secret filming is not the camera that is being used; it is whether the subject of filming realises they are being recorded.

For example, in the United States at an Oakland (California) train station on New Year's Day in 2009,

22-year-old Oscar Grant was shot by a police officer while the event was being filmed at close range by a member of the public:

> What is most revealing and of particular interest here are the words of the camera operator as she realizes that Grant had been shot and as she simultaneously boards a train to leave the scene. She yells, 'Get on the train. They just shot him, they just shot that guy.' She then directs her voice away from her fellow citizens and to the police, yelling, 'I got you mother fuckers'... This is not passive or hidden observation as in the [Rodney] King video – this is a conscious and overt decision to record events for public distribution. In this sense, camera surveillance is employed as a form of civic engagement.[2]

The woman filming knew what she was doing. She knew the police officer was not conscious that he was being filmed. She knew she was capturing evidence of something that should never happen: a cold-blooded shooting of a civilian, who was lying face down on a train platform, by a police officer.

Again and again, police officers have been filmed by mobile or cellular telephones – without the police officer realising.

Also in the United States, in April 2015, a police officer, Michael Slager, fired eight shots at 50-year-old Walter Scott in South Carolina. It was reported all over the world because footage of the incident was filmed on a phone:

> Following the shooting on Saturday, Officer Slager, 33, filed a police report defending his actions, saying

he feared for his life and Scott wrestled his Taser gun from him during a scuffle which broke out after he pulled over the 50-year-old for a broken brake light.

Four days later, Mr Santana's explosive video was made public – and blew the cop's story wide open.

Mr Santana told Today that Scott, a U.S. Coast Guard veteran and father-of-four, 'was trying to get away from the Taser... He never grabbed the Taser from the police.'

Slager was charged with Scott's murder on Tuesday and could face the death penalty.[3]

Feidin Santana, a 23-year-old barber, told the police he had a video of the incident but then ran for it, fearing reprisals, and anonymously handed the footage to the media.

It is not just in the United States that footage filmed on phones is holding the police to account.

In the UK, a national newspaper reported the experience of Tilly Gifford, a climate-change activist and protestor. In 2009, Strathclyde police interviewed Gifford twice. They were trying to recruit her as an informer, even though the group she was part of is peaceful and law-abiding.

Gifford recorded those meetings, secretly using 'a mobile phone and device sewn into her waistcoat to record what they described as a "business proposal" that she should think of as a job'.[4]

The audio she recorded was published in *The Guardian* newspaper. Her work lifted the lid on how far the police were willing to go – and how much they were willing to pay – to infiltrate even peaceful, law-abiding groups of protestors.

Juliana Napier, Tilly Gifford and Dan Glass with
some of the recording equipment they used.
Source: Copyright © Murdo MacLeod

It is not just the police who are filmed secretly using mobile or cellular telephones.

In the United States, groups of women identified perverts and prevented them from carrying out their intrusions, using only the cameras in their phones:

> The day that a man was caught masturbating on the subway was the day that the women of New York said enough was enough. ...a disgusted fellow passenger took a picture of the man with her camera phone and posted it on the internet... Inspired by her use of technology, one woman and six friends launched a website that invites people who have been sexually

harassed in public to take a picture of the offender and post it online, thus shaming the guilty party.[5,6]

To drive home the point: almost anything is possible with a mobile or cellular telephone if someone is prepared and sensible. It's not any one sector where they are being used and it is not just the English-speaking world that is seeing the impact of cameras in phones. For example, in Finland, a member of the public used their mobile phone to film two security guards beating a man in 2006. One of them was convicted as a result of this mobile phone footage:

> ...a passer-by secretly filmed the assault with a camera phone and posted the footage on YouTube. The clip first shows how one security guard beat the man with a baton before the man was arrested – the man had previously tried to hit the security guard with his fist. What then followed was subsequently heavily debated: the other security guard kicked the arrested man twice in the back, while he lay on his stomach on the ground with his hands tied in handcuffs behind him.[7]

Another author, Hille Koskela, wrote about that incident:

> The guards who were supposed to protect the public were committing a crime, a passer-by who is supposed to be protected as a member of the public took care of the surveillance work, and the police appeared as outsiders until the last minute... It seems the authorities cannot control how and where surveillance is used...the use of surveillance has slid from the private *sector* to private *individuals*... Wherever new forms of technology arise, new forms of resistance and alternative implementation are created.[8]

I have found myself using my phone more and more as a recording device, and the more frequently I use it, the more natural it becomes. For example, I frequently use my phone when I am doing surveillance work, just to get an additional angle.

Despite all those 'proper' secret cameras, it is just more effective sometimes to use the camera in my phone, held steady and sideways, pointed at one or other of the reverse mirrors in my car. Because I can move the phone and I can see what I am doing, I can film better shots than the more fixed 'proper' cameras.

Mobile or cellular telephones are bringing cameras into situations across the world that need to be filmed. Their versatility and omnipresence is placing them at the forefront of secret filming by members of the public.

NOTES

1. The Network for Police Monitoring (Netpol) (2012) 'A rough guide to filming the police during a stop & search.' Available at http://netpol. org/2012/07/27/a-rough-guide-to-filming-the-police-during-a-stop-search, accessed on 29 July 2014.

2. Finn, J. (2012) Seeing Surveillantly: Surveillance as Social Practice. In A. Doyle, R. Lippert and D. Lyon (eds) *Eyes Everywhere: The Global Growth of Camera Surveillance* (pp.76–77). London: Routledge.

3. Boyle, L. and Spargo, C. (2015) '"I ran": Killer cop witness tells how he fled the scene in fear after he told officers he had an incriminating video – and almost deleted the footage because he was afraid for his own life.' Available at www.dailymail.co.uk/news/article-3031326/ Witness-filmed-Walter-Scott-murder-breaks-silence-describing-emotional-moment-gave-video-victim-s-family-fundraising-site-SUPPORTING-killer-cop-continues-receive-donations.html, accessed on 22 August 2015.

4.   Lewis, P. (2009) 'Police caught on tape trying to recruit Plane Stupid protester as spy.' Available at www.theguardian.com/uk/2009/apr/24/strathclyde-police-plane-stupid-recruit-spy, accessed on 5 July 2014.

5.   Smith, D. (2006) 'Mobile vigilantes snap sex pests in action.' Available at www.theguardian.com/technology/2006/apr/30/news.theobserver, accessed on 27 July 2015.

6.   The 'hollaback' movement has since expanded to 84 cities and 31 countries; see www.ihollaback.org, accessed on 2 October 2015.

7.   Mallén, A. (2012) Citizen Journalism, Surveillance and Control. Originally published in G.V. Walle, N. Zurawski and E. Van den Herrewegen (eds) *Crime, Security and Surveillance: Effects for the Surveillant and the Surveilled* (p.5). The Hague: Boom/Eleven International Publishing. Available at www.academia.edu/2416955/Citizen_Journalism_Surveillance_and_Control, accessed on 23 June 2014.

8.   Koskela, H. (2009) Hijacking Surveillance? The New Moral Landscapes of Amateur Photographing. In K.F. Aas, H.O. Gundhus and H.M. Lomell (eds) *Technologies of Insecurity: The Surveillance of Everyday Life* (p.148). Abingdon: Routledge-Cavendish.

Chapter 4

DO YOU REALLY HAVE TO?

Ethical Dilemmas: Privacy, the Public Interest and Deception

The main challenges that people doing secret filming in future will face are not technical – they are ethical. Anyone considering infringing on someone's privacy or deceiving someone else should have a long hard think first. What gives them the right to film another person without that person's knowledge?

There are significant differences between the ethics involved with what a journalist like me does and what happens when a member of the public takes up cameras. For a start, even though professionals like me are governed by extensive guidelines and carefully monitored, we are always essentially outsiders invading someone else's privacy and intending to broadcast what we film, if appropriate. There is less room to criticise people for secret filming given that they might not even publish what they record. It really might be kept private, as a lot of people decide not broadcast their secret footage.

THE APPROVAL NEEDED FOR SECRET FILMING AT THE BBC, FROM THE BBC'S EDITORIAL GUIDELINES[1]

» Any proposal to carry out secret recording must be referred to Editorial Policy prior to approval by the relevant senior editorial figure in the division or, for independents, by the commissioning editor.

» The gathering and broadcast of secretly recorded material is always a two-stage process, requiring a justification for any intrusion at each stage. So, the decision to gather is always taken separately from the decision to transmit.

» A record must be kept of the approval process, even if the request is turned down or the material gathered isn't broadcast. Each division is responsible for maintaining its own secret recording records to enable the BBC to monitor and review its use across all output.

» Any deception required to obtain secretly recorded material (beyond the concealing of recording equipment) should be the minimum necessary and proportionate to the subject matter and must be referred to the relevant senior editorial figure or, for independents, to the commissioning editor.

People often film wrongdoing that happens to occur right in front of them – for example, a police officer or security guard assaulting someone. The person doing the filming in those cases has not sought the events they film. Something happens, it is wrong and someone films it.

Other people who take up secret cameras usually are motivated by concerns about their own safety or the treatment of someone they love. Often they are filming on their own property or where they have a personal concern. As a result, their dilemmas are more immediate than for professional journalists like me.

However, as long as those provisos are kept in mind, my experience can still help people decide whether to use cameras in future. In 2003, a film-maker, investigative journalist and friend of mine named Andy Head was contacted by a number of people worried about the safety of their relatives in a local psychiatric hospital. This was when I was working for Andy for regional BBC television. At the time, I was still wearing hidden cameras myself, going undercover in a range of settings.

Those families said their loved ones, who had been committed to this hospital as a place of safety under the UK Mental Health Act or who had voluntarily entered this hospital because they needed protection, had wandered out of the supposed 'place of safety' (as it is legally designated). One family – of a patient at the hospital – told us their relative had died as a result of walking out unnoticed.

There were other concerns as well; for example, allegedly patients were not being kept safe, were receiving little treatment and paperwork was being faked. We decided that we had to investigate.

Going undercover in a psychiatric hospital would see me following in the footsteps of one of my heroes from the history of covert investigations, 'Nellie Bly' (see 'Undercover Tales' at the end of this chapter).

Before I went to seek a job, we considered carefully whether it was justified. We would be invading privacy in a medical environment, but also we knew it would be such a lot of work. It would be a huge commitment of resources.

We decided that I would seek the job, but at first without wearing secret cameras, so that our invasion of privacy would be as limited as possible at least until we had confirmed that things were as bad as we had been told. At the BBC our guidelines are intended to ensure that we always try to carefully judge not only whether we are doing the right thing, but whether we are doing it in the right way.

The psychiatric hospital looked beautiful. It was a red-brick mansion on sprawling country grounds on top of a cliff, overlooking the ocean and nearby towns. There was something of the Victorian asylum, the house on the hill where no one goes – except the ill and those paid to tend to them.

The nurses and doctors did speak to a few patients, but it appeared to me that health care assistants – essentially untrained ward helpers – were the only ones who had contact with the majority of patients on any given day. One of the nurses took me outside as company while he had a cigarette.

'The same guy you see today will be back in a month,' he said.

This nurse told me that he had started out working at the hospital full of passion. As he sucked the last of his cigarette before throwing it down and crossing his arms, he said that the patients were right: there was no time, no money, no cures – just government initiatives and young nurses keen to make their career while older nurses, like him, felt tired and jaded.

Psychiatrists, nurses and health care assistants all said they had no time to interact with patients. The exceptions I saw were a student nurse who almost insisted on a one-to-one session with one patient, and once or twice when someone insisted, 'Come on, let's go sit in the lounge with the patients.' That was an exception; maybe like the older nurse had said – young and eager?

Mentally ill people coming in, being given drugs and going back out. It appeared to me over just a few shifts that maybe half of the patients were getting no 'talking cures'; they were being left to the tender mercies of kids like me with a day's training in restraint techniques and little or no knowledge of mental illness.

The conditions were immeasurably better than in the Victorian hospital to which 'Nellie Bly' got herself committed. She saw patients shackled or struck or forced into cold baths, screaming for all to hear. I did not see any members of staff who appeared to believe patients deserved cruelty or mistreatment, but I did see people ignored, not protected, and I heard patients claim they were taking recreational drugs on the wards.

I watched people who had been trained to provide care filling out forms in an office, day after day. As a result, often no one knew where patients were, and recreational drug use was alleged to be rife.

One day, I found one patient sitting downstairs curled up next to the drinks vending machine. I asked if he was OK, and he said, 'Yeah, I'm fine. Can't sit up there. I'm leaving tomorrow. I was bad when I came in.'

He was silent, letting that sink in, thinking back. 'I'm better now, but no thanks to here. You never see the doctor.

He's buried under a mountain of paperwork. He might see four patients every few days. The nurses are almost as bad. They're just in the office and they pick up on every new idea that comes along. They say you can see them whenever you want, but they're too busy. So you just sit there. You watch TV and smoke. I got better. I had a rest, but there's nothing up there. There's people getting worse up there. I'm leaving tomorrow.'

At that stage, we still had not been filming. I was there as an observer, checking whether the allegations our sources had made appeared to be right and still ongoing on the actual wards.

So now, having seen what I had seen, Andy Head and I had to decide what to do. We had to decide whether we should put hidden cameras in a hospital ward.

THE ETHICAL DILEMMA: SHOULD WE USE SECRET CAMERAS?

The evidence I saw first-hand in that hospital could help explain why people's loved ones were getting hurt and not being protected. Faced by this evidence after just a few shifts, Andy and I discussed whether to start covertly filming everything that I was seeing.

These decisions are often messy: Andy and I argued about it, back and forth. I was young and all het up by what I was seeing. The need to protect and treat patients better was all too apparent, but I was also aware that the patients, who were only fighting or taking recreational drugs because they were so bored, were going to be filmed in order to prove the wrongdoing of care workers.

The patients would in effect be caught in the crossfire. One patient had extreme delusions. He was convinced he was constantly being filmed by secret cameras. Covertly recording him could make that fear reality. I could not consult the patients directly to ask how they would feel about being filmed or else we would blow the whole operation. We had to gauge whether they would be in favour of our filming if we could have told them.

Given the almost universal discontent I was hearing from them about their perceived lack of any treatment, other than medication, it was reasonable to think they might support us, but it really was a tricky question. Could they be expected to approve?

The calculation was not only whether what we were seeing was wrong, but also whether any of the elements of wrongdoing I was seeing could be evidenced sufficiently clearly by other means. We were asking ourselves, 'Is it bad enough to justify filming the patients as well as the staff?'

Many readers will be aware that this kind of debate is often discussed in terms of whether something is in 'the public interest', which is a much-debated term, and I do not pretend to have the final word (the reader can explore the consideration of privacy and justification as given by authors Roy Greenslade and Stephen Whittle for further analysis[2]). For the layperson, the point is that there should be a jolly good reason for using a secret camera because there is always a trade-off, and the greater the invasion of privacy, the better the reasons for filming must be.

The public interest: the British perspective

I found one study particularly helpful when considering how different groups understand the public interest. A team of British researchers in 2002 examined the public interest and invasion of privacy. They interviewed media professionals, regulators and campaigners and carried out focus groups. They also conducted a national survey.

That study found all groups agreed that someone's right to privacy depends on where that person was. The authors said there are 'three types of space wherein expectations to privacy differed. They were: Closed space (the home); Restricted public space (the office or secluded beach); Open public space (town centre, shopping precincts, open public beach).'

In any of those spaces there needs to be sufficient justification to invade someone's privacy, but the more private somewhere is, the greater the justification would need to be. The public interest also had to be balanced against the extent of the negative impact of revelations on someone.

That much the people interviewed agreed on, but deciding how much justification is required in any given situation and even what 'the public interest' means is more complicated: 'there did not seem to be any one firm definition of the term'.[3]

One of the men who wrote the BBC's current editorial policy guidelines, Roger Mahony, told me that a session at the recent British inquiry into bad behaviour by the tabloid press (the 'Leveson Inquiry'[4]) praised the BBC's definition of 'the public interest'. Roger said that Lord Justice Leveson commended the BBC's understanding of the basis for saying a particular action was for the greater good.

Someone presented with that fact could be surprised that the BBC was praised if they know that the BBC's definition of 'public interest' is in fact almost the same as the definition used by the largely discredited Press Complaints Commission. The significant difference, Roger Mahony explained, was that the BBC's definition included *proportionality*. The BBC has set itself the task of judging not just whether something is important or of interest to the public, but also whether the badness being exposed is *sufficiently* bad to merit the methods being employed to gather evidence.

In other words, currently, the key question for a member of the public debating whether or not to carry out their own secret filming is not just 'Is whatever you want to film wrong?' but also 'Is the bad thing you want to film *bad enough* to justify the level of intrusion you are suggesting?'

Is there sufficient evidence to justify filming? Were there enough complaints first to conclude there are no other options? People doing their own secret filming need to be ready to mull and to challenge their own assumptions. Roger Mahony stated:

> There is lots of secret filming. It's not just what ends up on *Panorama*. If you read local papers, there is lots of secret filming, sometimes even just on people's mobile phones or recording phone calls, and it does get results.
>
> The big question one could consider is: If you are filming someone and not seeing anything worrying, do you want masses of footage of someone without them knowing they are being filmed? That's when, if you were caught, you would feel more uncomfortable. Are we still justified? Is what we're doing proportional

to the wrong we're uncovering? Is it a lot of filming for little evidence?

The key, Roger said, is really trying to avoid 'using a hammer to smash a nut'.

IS 'THE PUBLIC INTEREST' THE RIGHT TEST FOR PEOPLE DOING THEIR OWN FILMING IN FUTURE?

Someone reading this book might be debating whether or not to use secret cameras to film possible mistreatment of their loved one. Someone in that position might argue that I am setting too high a bar for people doing their own filming. My father asked whether 'the public interest' is even relevant given someone using secret cameras might well be filming their own family member or even their own experiences. He questioned whether in those cases there is a lower bar that might be called 'the private interest' that would be sufficient. After all, someone might say, 'It is my mum, so why shouldn't I film her?'

It is a reasonable question, particularly when members of the public are not setting out to publish or broadcast what they record.

The key question for me, however, is whether a vulnerable person – even if it *is* someone's mother – knows they are being filmed.

I have no objection if someone chooses to put up security cameras in their garage or around their house: houses and garages do not have a right to privacy. I do not think that being someone's child (or someone's parent) gives you absolute rights over them. John Locke wrote, 'The power, then, that parents have over their children, arises from that duty which is incumbent on them, to take care of their off-spring, during the imperfect state of childhood.'[5] The reverse is true, I would suggest, when parents arrive at a similar 'imperfect state' and need assistance.

Do not get me wrong. Caring children are usually better placed to assess their parents' interests than anyone else, and I think the view of demonstrably loving carers trumps pretty much anyone else's view, but it is still important to consider whether any vulnerable person would approve of the filming if it were safe for them to know what was going on. If the person being filmed would not approve, if they would not feel the issues being filmed justified the intrusion, then that seems to me a problem, regardless of who is putting in a camera.

Back at that psychiatric hospital, there is no question in my mind given the scale of the really poor practice and even bad behaviour we were seeing that we had good reason to carry out secret filming. However, even though it would have been reasonable (or 'proportionate') to secretly film them in any other context, we were still agonising about filming them because it was in the most private place: a hospital environment. It was a tough dilemma, one that might have gone either way.

The answer may well have been 'yes' or it could have been 'no'. We will never know.

As it happened, Andy and I were spared the final decision. Events overtook us and so we never used hidden cameras inside that psychiatric hospital.

Someone who knew me as a journalist was admitted as a patient. She walked into the small ward canteen of the psychiatric hospital on the first night of her third admittance. The problem was that this woman knew exactly who I was. Not long before, I had openly filmed with her husband for a different film.

If she had said, 'I know you, you are a journalist', it actually could have been quite dangerous. I did not want to get unmasked in the midst of a crowd, many of whom could feel betrayed and some of whom were quiet volatile. There was not much alternative because I also really did not want to call her a liar falsely. So, I ducked below the counter, just leaving my hand up with her food, which she took from me without seeing me before wandering back to her table. I then raced out of the canteen and made sure I was busy elsewhere. That was my last shift. I stopped working at the hospital.

In the end, we made the film a different way, filming only *outside* the hospital.

In general, with this kind of work, we need to *be able* to film everywhere, but that does not mean that we need to *actually* film everywhere. Cameras up in every room and every institution can obscure the evidence we are trying to collect. It can become a tidal wave, a white noise. Worse yet, it could drive bad behaviour into darker corners – whether that is directly under cameras or in the broom cupboard.

There is some evidence that members of the public accept instinctively that there should be a reason before you film someone secretly. In 2003, *Parenting* magazine and an *America Online* survey of nearly 4000 mothers in the United States found:

> 82 percent said they would secretly videotape their nanny not only if they suspected their children were not receiving proper care and attention, but also to protect their caregivers from false accusations of abuse. Some said they would resort to videotaping only if they suspected abuse. Otherwise, they said, it was unethical to use cameras secretly. Although 18 percent of respondents said they objected to using hidden surveillance, some admitted they had videotaped their caregivers – only not in secret.[6]

There are also practical reasons to restrict the amount of secret filming to the bare minimum, to the times when it is absolutely unavoidable, as it can take a terrible toll on the people involved, damaging their relationships and causing them stress (more on this in Chapter 6).

THE ETHICAL DILEMMA FACED BY MEMBERS OF THE PUBLIC

Members of the public are too often having to overcome the same ethical dilemmas Andy and I had, but without advice or support.

That can lead to terrible results. At the very worst, there are examples of covert recording by members of the public where there is just no possible justification – for example, a gynaecologist who misused his position of trust: 'The doctor wore an unusual pen around his neck. It was really a concealed camera, and for years he secretly recorded women at some of their most private moments, during pelvic exams.'[7] That doctor's misdeeds cost Johns Hopkins Hospital in the United States more than $190 million in damages in July 2014.

Too often it can be the same when people take photos or record footage with their phones:

> ...[one] sketchy analysis of the 100 latest readers' mobile phone pictures on the website of a Finnish free tabloid, Uutislehit 100, showed that one-third of the pictures published showed traffic accidents, fires or witnessed crime scenes...this amateur imagery is reminiscent of 'pornography'.[8]

The difference can feel paper-thin sometimes. One of the two journalists who secretly recorded Prime Minister Harold Wilson after he left office,[9] Roger Courtiour, pointed out to me that it is the same instinct – often considered only briefly – that causes people to record bad behaviour by police officers as causes them to record other things that are less worthwhile, that are just 'of interest' to people. Too much filming, in his view, by professionals and the general public is not of things that are genuinely in the public interest. 'Sometimes people film knowing they are going to get important evidence. That is the best sort of civic surveillance. But then there is voyeuristic filming, like when people point their phone at a car crash,' Roger told me.

Since 2014, I have twice been approached by people considering secret filming, where I was concerned by what they were telling me – but where, far from turning it into a television programme, I realised that I had to talk them out of using hidden cameras. Their concerns were real, but the evidence just was not yet strong enough.

Frustrated, they both separately suggested secretly recording their friends to get evidence that other people shared the same concerns. I had to explain that their friends, in each case, were not the 'bad guys'. They were worried other people were doing bad things, but now they wanted to film their friends talking about the same fears, without the permission of those friends.

One needs to know when one is invading someone's privacy by secretly filming them, and one needs to be clear about why one is doing it. Anyone who wants to record their friend is not focusing on the real issue. I understand why someone uses hidden cameras after they have seen bruises or if they have seen bad attitudes in a care home, and after they have made complaints which have been ignored. Without that evidence, though, and those previous actions, secret filming is neither justified nor proportionate. However, sometimes covert filming is the only ethical and sensible response to wrongdoing. Across society, the same truth applies: hidden cameras are too often necessary and sadly will continue to be the last weapon of truth when all else has failed. Where those conditions are achieved and secret filming has been carefully considered before, during and after it is done, the people doing it deserve and need to be supported.

NOTES

1.   BBC (2015) *Editorial Guidelines, Section 7: Privacy.* Available at www.bbc.co.uk/editorialguidelines/guidelines/privacy/secret-recording, accessed on 26 November 2015.

2.   See, for example, Cooper, G. and Whittle, S. (2008) *Privacy, Probity and Public Interest*. Available at http://reutersinstitute.politics.ox.ac.uk/publication/privacy-probity-and-public-interest, accessed on 28 July 2015.

3.   Morrison, D.E. and Svennevig, M. (2002) *The public interest, the media and privacy*. Available at www.ofcom.org.uk/static/archive/bsc/pdfs/research/pidoc.pdf, accessed on 17 January 2015.

4.   See, for example, www.bbc.co.uk/news/uk-20539192, accessed on 28 July 2015.

5.   Locke, J. (1690) *Second Treatise of Civil Government* (section 58); also quoted in a very accessible analysis: Gonick, L. (2007) *The Cartoon History of the Modern World* (pp.226–229). New York, NY: Harper Collins.

6.   Burson, P. (2005) 'Use of "nanny cams" raises issues of ethics, parents' rights.' Available at http://archive.azcentral.com/families/articles/0119videotaping19.html, accessed on 28 July 2015.

7.   Gabriel, T. (2014) 'Hospital Agrees to Pay $190 Million Over Recording of Pelvic Exams.' *The New York Times*, 21 July 2014.

8.   Koskela, H. (2009) Hijacking Surveillance? The New Moral Landscapes of Amateur Photographing. In K.F. Aas, H.O. Gundhus and H.M. Lomell (eds) *Technologies of Insecurity: The Surveillance of Everyday Life* (p.160). Abingdon: Routledge-Cavendish.

9.   See Chapter 1 for a more detailed discussion of Roger Courtiour and his investigation.

UNDERCOVER TALES

Victorian Infiltrations:
Heroes and Anti-Heroes

Queen Victoria's reign saw both the first undercover journalists and policemen using undercover tactics, but their covert or secret investigations did not involve the use of cameras.

Throughout the history of covert infiltration there has been an essential truth: either someone's reasons for deceiving another person and for invading their privacy are justified or they are not. Even in the early nineteenth century, some Victorian investigations were worthwhile and done well, but some were done badly.

Any invasion of someone's privacy under false pretences needs to be proportionate to the wrongdoing being exposed. That was just as true in the nineteenth century when there were not film cameras.

In 1887, a 23-year-old woman named Elizabeth Cochrane was hired by the *New York World* newspaper to investigate allegations of mistreatment at the women's lunatic asylum for the city, nearby on Blackwell's Island. Even though she did her journalism with typewriters and typeset, not cameras and television, she still had to assess whether deception was required – that is, whether it was justified.

The people who hired her were worried about reports that inmates were being given rotten food and freezing baths, and that some were even being beaten. To prove it, though, they would need someone to get inside.

Elizabeth Jane Cochrane (aka 'Nellie Bly')

Cochrane had to decide whether the very real personal risk was worth it. To pull it off, she would have to convince doctors that she was mad and infiltrate the asylum. If she was caught and revealed to be a journalist while trapped behind locked asylum doors, she would be at the mercy of her captors. Plus, by lying and sneaking on to Blackwell's

Island, she would be spying on vulnerable women, all of them trapped, some terribly ill, without their consent.

It is the same dilemma that I faced when I first went undercover for a long period of time, working undercover in an animal sanctuary. I was there to expose the abuse and unnecessary deaths of birds. In future it will be the same set of questions that will face anyone looking now at a secret camera and worried about their loved ones or themselves or a vulnerable person. Is it (whatever is thought to be going on) truly bad enough to justify the intrusion being proposed? What are the risks? Will it be safe, or at least safe *enough*? Will it be legal?

Cochrane agreed to feign madness, and she succeeded. She was admitted to Blackwell's Island, and under the pen name 'Nellie Bly' wrote a series of articles that exposed the terrible conditions in which those New York women were living, locked away from view.[1]

Her revelations are still stomach-churning today. Although Victorian abuse was often more public and on show than abuse today, reading the revelations reported by 'Nellie' will be too familiar for comfort for people who have watched the abuse that some of my films have revealed.

In poorly regulated or managed and closed settings, barbarity can flourish. One of the deputy editors at the BBC's *Panorama* programme, Frank Simmonds, says, 'Morality is what you do when you think no one is watching.'

'Nellie Bly' revealed patients who were cold, hungry and even mistreated. In this excerpt she describes one upset patient being handled by staff:

> She grew more hysterical every moment until they pounced upon her and slapped her face and knocked her head in a lively fashion. This made the poor creature cry the more, and so they choked her. Yes,

actually choked her. Then they dragged her out to the closet, and I heard her terrified cries hush into smothered ones. After several hours' absence she returned to the sitting-room, and I plainly saw the marks of their fingers on her throat for the entire day.

This punishment seemed to awaken their desire to administer more. They returned to the sitting-room and caught hold of an old gray-haired woman whom I have heard addressed both as Mrs. Grady and Mrs. O'Keefe. She was insane, and she talked almost continually to herself and to those near her. She never spoke very loud, and at the time I speak of was sitting harmlessly chattering to herself. They grabbed her, and my heart ached as she cried:

'For God sake, ladies, don't let them beat me.'

'Shut up, you hussy!' said Miss Grady as she caught the woman by her gray hair and dragged her shrieking and pleading from the room. She was also taken to the closet, and her cries grew lower and lower, and then ceased.

The nurses returned to the room and Miss Grady remarked that she had 'settled the old fool for awhile.' I told some of the physicians of the occurrence, but they did not pay any attention to it...[2]

Without a camera or proof beyond her own testimony, the articles by 'Nellie Bly' (which were collected eventually into a book titled *Ten Days in a Mad-House*) changed the way the mentally ill were treated in America. Elizabeth Cochrane's work was a landmark in the reform of Victorian psychiatric warehouses across the world.

VERDICT: 'NELLIE BLY' WAS JUSTIFIED.

INFILTRATION AND INVESTIGATION IS NOT EASY, EVEN IF YOU GET STRONG EVIDENCE

Although it is clear now that Elizabeth Cochrane made the right decision by infiltrating a hospital, at the time she was challenged over her actions and had to defend them in front of a grand jury. There was an inspection which found no problems, but 'Nellie' challenged them, pointing out she understood the psychiatric hospital was warned they would be visited – unlike when she had snuck in as a patient and seen how the institution really operated. She wrote the following in a postscript to that article when it was republished in book form:

> I hardly expected the grand jury to sustain me, after they saw everything different from what it had been while I was there. Yet they did, and their report from court advises all the changes made that I had proposed. I have one consolation for my work – on the strength of my story the committee of appropriation provides $1,000,000 more than was ever before given, for the benefit of the insane.[3]

That same dynamic is as relevant now as in Cochrane's time. Secret filming is held up to scrutiny today in the same way that investigation was back then. For example, people who were involved in films I worked on four years ago are still giving evidence to hearings or else facing other questions and complaints about their actions. Just as Elizabeth Cochrane needed to face a grand jury, anyone who takes up cameras and starts filming people had better be ready to face unknown legal and investigatory processes. Everyone involved had better be ready to explain why they did what they did.

Not all secret filming today is worthwhile, and not all Victorian undercover investigation was good. There were ignoble investigations in the same era as 'Nellie Bly' (again, even before secret cameras were invented).

A protest group called the Legitimation League was formed in 1895 in England and was dedicated to pressing for the rights of children born out of wedlock. Victorian England denied such babies many legal rights and labelled their mothers 'harlots'. This caught the eye of the authorities. Inspector G. Sweeney infiltrated the Legitimation League. So intent was Inspector Sweeney on ending what he called 'a growing evil in the shape of a vigorous campaign of free love and Anarchism'[4] that even when he did not find any illegal activity by members of the League, he in effect 'fitted up' the leading organiser George Bedborough, arresting him for nothing worse than that the League had distributed a book deemed pornographic at the time.

These actions were disproportionate: if the authorities had been aiming to prevent pornographers from plying their trade, there were many more worthy targets than George Bedborough.

Just as Elizabeth Cochrane's investigation sets the bar for invasion of privacy based on firm evidence and it being carried out for the greater good, Sweeney's investigation marks a nadir. It is absolutely possible to misuse either infiltration or (later, once it was invented) secret recording equipment.

VERDICT: INSPECTOR SWEENEY WAS NOT JUSTIFIED.

The techniques employed by 'Nellie' remain relevant today, as they are the forebear of both the modern investigations into care that I have conducted and also the efforts of many families to film their relatives' care. However, the sometimes dubious techniques employed by Inspector Sweeney have modern echoes as well when police officers today still go too far in their undercover investigations. A series of undercover police officers have been exposed in recent years – we have learned that they have gone way beyond any defensible subterfuge to find out about the activities of sometimes even peaceful protestors.[5]

NOTES

1. Bly, N. [Cochrane Seaman, Elizabeth Jane] (1887) *Ten Days in a Mad-House*. New York, NY: Ian L. Munro, Publisher. Available at http:// digital.library.upenn.edu/women/bly/madhouse/madhouse.html, accessed on 28 July 2015.

2. Bly, N. [Cochrane Seaman, Elizabeth Jane] (1887) *Ten Days in a Mad-House* (Chapter XIII).

3. Bly, N. [Cochrane Seaman, Elizabeth Jane] (1887) *Ten Days in a Mad-House* (Chapter XVII).

4. Bunyan, T. (1976) *The History and Practice of the Political Police in Britain*. London: Julian Friedmann Publishers.

5. See, for example, Bracchi, P. (2011) *As a third police officer is exposed for sleeping with the enemy, we reveal the reckless excesses of the 'under covers' squad*. Available at www.dailymail.co.uk/news/article-1349445/A-undercover-police-officers-exposed-sleeping-enemy.html, accessed on 18 April 2015.

Chapter 5

DO PEOPLE GET IN TROUBLE?

Secret Filming and the Law

A talented young undercover reporter named Tamanna Rahman filmed people (including children) racially abusing and threatening her in 2009. There were good people on the two different Bristol housing estates where she filmed, but there were small groups who felt free to abuse her, throw stones at her head and call her terrible names. A young man punched her colleague, Amil Khan, who was undecover with her, in the head. Tamanna and Amil were secretly filming everything that happened to them, wearing hidden cameras. Their footage was featured in a film for the BBC's *Panorama* programme produced by Karen Wightman (I was the assistant producer) called *Hate on the Doorstep*.

It was an extreme assignment. Tamanna Rahman had to learn not to flinch, even when she was in danger. When she first walked out on those streets wearing cameras, understandably she would often jump or be startled when someone threw something at her or shouted at her. That meant that the cameras she was wearing picked up nothing at the critical moment except for spinning air and swirling colours. Eventually, she learned to remain perfectly still even when terrible things were happening around her and near her. Tamanna wrote the following at the time:

> On my second day on the estate I had a rock thrown towards me as I returned from a shopping trip. I was called 'Paki' and had obscenities muttered at me as I walked by. This from people who knew nothing about me. Over the course of our investigation I would have glass, a can, a bottle and stones thrown at me.[1]

Tamanna Rahman and Amil Khan
Source: BBC (2009) Panorama: Undercover: Hate on the Doorstep. BBC1, 19 October (20:30 hrs). Copyright © BBC

Housing estates on the outskirts of many British towns and cities got little of the money which poured into 'inner city renewal' during the decades before that film. The residents of those poorer communities – like poor people across Britain – were some of those most exposed by the credit boom (cheap loans and hire purchase schemes) and the worst ravages of the 2008 economic collapse. People felt forgotten. Community ties were slackening. There were some people on the main housing estate where Tamanna lived who were kind or smiled at her, though most people didn't react at all, but it was clear that the behaviour of young people and the controls on them had slipped loose. 'Foreigners' were too easy a target for that wildness.

After Tamanna switched off her secret cameras, we delivered letters to everyone we intended to identify in our final programme. To our surprise, the mother of one of the children Tamanna had secretly filmed being abusive took our letter straight to Avon and Somerset Constabulary, the local police force. (I could be wrong, but I suspect that mother thought Tamanna had broken the law by filming her son.) Her son was promptly taken in for questioning by the police after they'd read our letter.

Every time someone uses a secret camera, they believe that they could capture evidence of an antisocial or illegal act, but the subject of filming may disagree about who is breaking the law. As in the case of that mother in Bristol, the person who is being filmed may feel that the real issue is their privacy being invaded – or, in other cases, that someone trespassed on their property.

Karen Wightman and I planned that investigation carefully. We arranged several meetings with the BBC's tip-top in-house lawyers, some of the most experienced folk in the business. We talked through the logistics of the different activities our reporters would need to do and the different legal hurdles we might face.

Similar but more extreme legal conversations and considerations were required when Karen and I decided to infiltrate the British Army by getting another, different undercover reporter, Russell Sharp, to become an infantry soldier. The number of potential laws which needed to be considered seemed to get longer with every meeting that passed when planning that investigation. (I have always needed independent legal advice. It would be impossible – and beyond my expertise – to offer either 'one-size-fits-all' legal guidance or advice. The balance between different rights and what laws might apply always depends on the specifics of an individual case.)

IS SECRET FILMING ILLEGAL IN THE UK?

The short answer is 'probably not'; however, anyone who is worried about their situation should get proper independent legal advice. The national regulator for health and social care in England, the Care Quality Commission, wrote the following in their advice on filming in care homes: 'Using recording equipment is new for most of us... We do not know of anyone who has used this equipment being taken to court as a result. However, the exact legal situation will vary in every case.'[2]

I completed a compulsory legal course for BBC staff which put the precedent related to care homes, for example, simply:

> ...in 2009 the operators of a care home tried unsuccessfully to get an injunction against the BBC to prevent the broadcast of a programme which revealed

> poor standards in its nursing home. A reporter had
> gone undercover and worked there, filming secretly.
> The judge held that it was 'firmly arguable' that the
> public interest justified the clandestine filming...[3]

Everyone usually has some expectation of privacy, but that is always balanced by other considerations – for example, by security concerns: intelligence agencies regularly breach their citizens' privacy, and where that is (for example) to tackle terrorist plots, much of society seems to tolerate it most of the time.

The expectation that people will be left alone as much as possible has evolved over centuries. In Britain, the Magna Carta in 1215 declared:

> No free man shall be seized or imprisoned, or stripped
> of his rights or possessions, or outlawed or exiled, or
> deprived of his standing in any other way, nor will we
> proceed with force against him, or send others to do
> so, except by the lawful judgement of his equals or by
> the law of the land.[4]

In the nineteenth century, John Stuart Mill demanded a wider set of rights than whether someone would be imprisoned or physically mistreated when he said, 'The liberty of the individual must be thus far limited; he must make himself a nuisance to other people.'[5] Mill encoded a sense that men (at least, at that time) should not find themselves constrained unless they negatively affect someone else. There has to be harm or at least nuisance before someone's liberty to do most anything should be constrained.

That cuts both ways. Preventing filming constrains one person, but being filmed without permission infringes on another's privacy. There is always a judgement to be made. When does filming, recording or capturing images of someone become a 'nuisance', in Mill's terms? When is there sufficient public interest to justify that invasion of privacy?

Article 8 of the European Convention on Human Rights states:

> Right to respect for private and family life.
>
> 1. Everyone has the right to respect for his private and family life, his home and his correspondence.
>
> 2. There shall be no interference by a public authority with the exercise of this right except such as is in accordance with the law and is necessary in a democratic society in the interests of national security, public safety or the economic well-being of the country, for the prevention of disorder or crime, for the protection of health or morals, or for the protection of the rights and freedoms of others.[6]

The Convention has been incorporated into British law, and privacy actions against journalists pursuing a range of different stories (not necessarily or particularly involving secret filming) are becoming more common. However, my personal experience of the impact of the law *on secret filming* to date is that while I once was threatened with privacy action, there was finally no lawsuit in actual fact. My experience is that while there are a number of laws that apply to covert recording (as below), I have never been sued for breach of privacy. Someone threatened me once but never actually did anything. However, I would like to think that the times I have used hidden cameras have been particularly justified, as they have been proportionate and thoroughly considered.

We are in a fast-changing legal environment. People using secret cameras in future and the people affected by secret cameras will consider their options and may need to get legal advice.

REGULATORS AND SOCIAL WORKERS TAKE NOTE

The legal context in this chapter is particularly important for professionals, particularly regulators and social workers, who are presented with or who become aware of covert recording. Too often, local authorities, social workers and regulators have seemed more concerned about privacy than protection. They can act as if the moral position is relative, as if everyone has a valid point. However, if someone has behaved badly and someone else has recorded unequivocal evidence of that wrongdoing, there is no equivalence: one person has mistreated someone and a second person is trying to stop it.

There are grounds for egregiously voyeuristic or invasive secret filming to be pursued by the police. For example, a 52-year-old man saw his phone destroyed and was sentenced in January 2015 to a three-year suspended sentence for the crime of 'outraging public decency' after he was caught in a British store, Poundland, taking photos up women's skirts.[7] However, assuming someone is not carrying out perverted and abusive intrusion, often the key legal question in practical terms is not whether they will be sued for *secretly filming*; instead, the key legal question, in my experience, has been whether and how someone *publishes* the results.

When I have received legal threats in the past about invasion of privacy, the concern was actually not about the fact that there had been secret filming in and of itself. The people writing to me were not saying, 'How dare you turn on a secret camera!' Instead, they said they were worried about the impact on someone's privacy of my *broadcasting* secret footage in a television programme. Dissemination, sharing and broadcasting or publication of secret footage can, depending on the circumstances, see someone in court faced with a number of different possible complaints. Someone in the UK could get sued for libel, for breach of confidentiality, for misuse of private information or potentially (in some circumstances) for breach of duty under the 1998 Data Protection Act – depending on what was involved.

If a person's photo is taken at a shopping mall and then is published online, they might be able theoretically to sue for something. It's unlikely, though, that they will bother. However, in different circumstances – say, if the person being photographed is the supermodel Naomi Campbell and she was walking out of a meeting composed of members of an anonymous self-help group – that calculation could shift.[8] Then there might be legal action depending on how the photo was taken, obtained, published and sold.

Judges' considerations in cases like that of Naomi Campbell, who did successfully sue over exactly such photos (and also of Max Mosley, the former president of the *Fédération Internationale de l'Automobile*, who brought proceedings against a national newspaper that published, without prior warning, covert pictures of his sadomasochistic romp with prostitutes[9]) have depended on issues such as whether there is sufficient 'public interest' balanced against someone's expectation of privacy. (See Chapter 4 for a detailed discussion of 'the public interest'.) Lord Hope in the case of *Naomi Campbell v Mirror Group Newspapers* stated:

> The underlying question in all cases where it is alleged that there has been a breach of duty of confidence is whether the information that was disclosed was private and not public...
>
> If the information is obviously private, the situation will be one where the person to whom it relates can reasonably expect his privacy to be respected.[10]

To take another example, the celebrity chef Gordon Ramsay's father-in-law was reported in the *Daily Mail* to have sued Ramsay for breach of privacy in 2012, after Ramsay allegedly hired a private eye who in turn took compromising photos of the father-in-law with his mistress[11] – and then threatened them with the photo during a family business dispute. Context is king in all these cases.

INTERNATIONAL COMPARISONS

Covert recording and the law varies from country to country. Sometimes it is more complicated or more legally risky than in the UK. There are nations with specific statutes prohibiting covert recording; for example, legislation in Australia varies according to territory. Secret filming can be a criminal act.

'Proper' secret cameras in the United States

The United States has precious little secret filming: more than once I have proposed covert recording in the United States and found people much more reluctant than in the UK. American journalists, charities and campaigners seem to start from an expectation that if they use covert recorders, they will have to defend themselves against privacy actions and other law suits.

The costs required to defend such cases can be prohibitive. Such calculations have a negative effect on the state of civil society, I would argue. They mean wrongdoing is allowed to continue. Even where mistreatment of vulnerable people is alleged in America, I usually won't be able to try to secretly film what is happening, to prove it. Abuse will be continuing right now because people cannot prove it is happening sufficiently robustly to drive real change.

The American system is not just litigious; it is also very complicated. Each state has such different statutes. For example, some states require that permission be obtained before anyone records a conversation or phone call (it's called 'two-party consent'[12]). As another example, California and New York differ massively on when it is legal to publish anything about someone without their permission.[13]

Given all those restrictions and constraints, I was flabbergasted to read that the same country has in some states in effect *protected* the rights of men to film up women's skirts without their permission even though this was clearly not the intention:

> ... California law holds that if a person can't be identified, 'there is no harm'. For example, Tyler Takehara, 50, of Pearl City, was charged with using a concealed camera

to shoot video up the skirts of unsuspecting women riding escalators at Ala Moana Center, but his attorney argued successfully it was not against the law... This position has been upheld by Washington State Supreme Court, overturning convictions of two men who took 'upskirt' photos to sell on the Internet.

New laws are being considered to address this problem...[14]

In effect, women's private parts are subject to being exposed on the Internet without their permission, while people with good intentions are being prevented from covertly filming in situations where there is suspicion of mistreatment in public institutions. I accept that this is not a totally fair comparison given there are states that have specific legal prohibitions against filming someone naked or through their clothes without their knowledge. Indeed, California has passed such legislation since that case,[15] and it is fair to point out that Tyler Takehara was pursued by the court, even though he was not convicted, so there is a will to pursue such actions. However, it remains true that certain states need to reconsider the balance they have struck between privacy and protection. The United States of America could benefit from more covert recording, in my view.

SECRET FILMING WITH CELLULAR TELEPHONES IN THE UNITED STATES

There is another side to secret filming in the United States. The use of a camera to record someone without their knowledge in a public place is not illegal – in fact, it's becoming increasingly common.[16] Many readers of this book will probably remember the footage filmed by Ramsey

Orta using his phone in Staten Island, a borough of New York City, in July 2014. He filmed a police officer placing an African American man, Eric Garner, in a chokehold – even though that method of restraint has been banned for years. The footage of Garner pleading 'I can't breathe' was watched all over the world. Garner died, and without that footage no one might have known the real reason, and there might have been no protests.

Ramsey Orta was indicted after that incident, but it was not (or at least was allegedly or ostensibly not) anything to do with breaching the police officers' privacy by filming the footage: Orta was charged because he allegedly hid a handgun in a teenage accomplice's waistband.[17]

THE LAW OF TRESPASS

Other laws – not related to privacy or publication – are relevant to secret filming, as well. 'Trespass' means going on to someone else's land without permission. Where that act is illegal or actionable varies around the world. In the UK, trespass is usually not a crime, unless someone is committing a mass trespass, is a hunt saboteur, is a squatter or is having a 'rave' (a boisterous dance party).[18] However, if one person sneaks on to someone else's property and installs a camera, then they could still be sued, under UK civil law, as a Parliamentary summary notes:

> Generally speaking, trespass to land is not a criminal offence unless some special statutory provision makes it so. Any damage done by a trespasser while trespassing may amount to the offence of criminal damage. In civil law, trespass to land consists of any unjustifiable intrusion by a person upon the land in

possession of another. Civil trespass is actionable in the courts.[19]

So it is possible that someone who commits trespass in order to carry out secret filming could be sued depending on where they are using cameras and why they are filming.

Even if someone is not actually sued, it is still worth considering whether the manner in which someone gains access in order to carry out filming might undermine the impact of their evidence.

For example, in 2011 in the UK, animal rights activists secretly filmed evidence of extreme cruelty. The owners of the abattoir in question were not prosecuted. The reason was the activists had snuck on to the property. The campaigners and many others were shocked by the decision, but despite evidence of apparent mistreatment, the Department for Environment, Food and Rural Affairs ('Defra') explained its reasoning to the *Daily Mail*:

> A Defra spokesman added: 'It would be totally irresponsible to prosecute when we know we'd lose,' saying that there were 'very strong legal grounds' not to prosecute hidden-camera cases.
>
> This is rejected by Animal Aid, which points out that the legal principle that allows prosecutions based on secret filming has already been established.
>
> For example, prosecutions are being brought against workers at a care home who were secretly filmed by the BBC's Panorama programme mistreating vulnerable residents...
>
> A spokesman [for Defra] said the footage at the slaughterhouse was obtained through trespass, while the Panorama filming was not.

He said: 'Animal cruelty is unacceptable, and we vigorously pursue action against accusations of cruelty wherever we can.

'It is wholly disingenuous to draw comparisons between this case and that of filming in a care home, because this video evidence was obtained unlawfully through trespass.

'As the RSPCA [Royal Society for the Prevention of Cruelty to Animals] has found in previous cases, this would get it thrown out of court and do absolutely nothing to help reduce the suffering of animals.'[20]

EVERY OTHER LAW

Whether people are taking up cameras (be they whistle-blowers, families or citizen journalists) or whether someone is concerned about secret filming, there is a final, slightly broader warning: other laws *could* apply. It just depends what exactly someone is proposing to film. One good example was pointed out to me by a friend. Three Canadian duck hunters knew they were being filmed (and in fact posted the footage on YouTube) when they blasted ducks out of a Saskatchewan pond in 2009. There were no privacy issues, they knew they were being filmed, but the men were hunting unlawfully, hunting out of season, discharging a firearm from a vehicle and leaving edible game to be wasted.[21] They were fined 5000 or 6000 Canadian dollars each and ordered to hand their rifles over to the authorities.

Depending on what is being filmed and how someone is behaving, any laws of the land – even local hunting regulations, or more often things like nuisance or harassment – could come into play, and so this discussion ends back where it started: some things are relatively straightforward, but I certainly get independent legal advice whenever I am in doubt about a particular bit of secret filming.

NOTES

1. Rahman, T. (2009) 'Reduced to a four-letter word.' Available at http://news.bbc.co.uk/panorama/hi/front_page/newsid_8303000/8303229.stm, accessed on 1 February 2015.

2. Care Quality Commission (2015) *Thinking about using a hidden camera or other equipment to monitor someone's care?* Available at www.cqc.org.uk/sites/default/files/20150212_public_surveillance_leaflet_final.pdf, accessed on 29 July 2015.

3. For more details, see BKM Limited vs British Broadcasting Corporation (2009) Mr Justice Mann in the High Court of Justice Chancery Division, 02/12/2009. Neutral Citation Number: [2009] EWHC 3151 (Ch). Case No: HC09C04462. Available at www.5rb.com/wp-content/uploads/2013/10/BKM-Ltd-v-BBC-2009-EWHC-3151-Ch.pdf, accessed on 29 April 2015.

4. King John (1215) *Magna Carta.* Original version available at www.bl.uk/treasures/magnacarta/index.html#, accessed on 29 July 2015.

5. Mill, J.S. (1859) On Liberty. Quoted in E. Knowles (ed.) (1999) *The Oxford Dictionary of Quotations* (p.508). Oxford: Oxford University Press.

6. European Convention on Human Rights (1998) *Human Rights Act.* Available at www.legislation.gov.uk/ukpga/1998/42/schedule/1, accessed on 29 July 2015.

7. BBC News (2015) '"Upskirt" voyeur Paul Appleby sentenced for 9,000 photos.' Available at www.bbc.co.uk/news/uk-england-northamptonshire-31002609, accessed on 28 January 2015.

8. Cooper, G. and Whittle, S. (2008) 'Privacy, probity and public interest.' Available at http://reutersinstitute.politics.ox.ac.uk/publication/privacy-probity-and-public-interest, accessed on 29 July 2015.

9. Melville-Brown, A. (2011) 'Max Mosley, the media and UK privacy laws.' Available at www.lawgazette.co.uk/analysis/max-mosley-the-

media-and-uk-privacy-laws/60541.fullarticle, accessed on 14 March 2015.

10. Opinions of the Lords of Appeal for Judgment in the Cause, Campbell (Appellant) v. MGN Limited (Respondents) on Thursday 6 May 2004. Available at www.publications.parliament.uk/pa/ld200304/ldjudgmt/jd040506/campbe-3.htm, accessed on 5 October 2015.

11. Gallagher, I. and Gould, L. (2012) 'I'll grill you in court: Ramsay sued by father-in-law's mistress over "secret filming" through bedroom window.' Available at www.dailymail.co.uk/news/article-2197006/Ill-grill-court-Ramsay-sued-father-laws-mistress-secret-filming-bedroom-window.html, accessed on 17 January 2015.

12. See The Reporters Committee for Freedom of the Press (2008) *Can we tape?* Available at www.rcfp.org/rcfp/orders/docs/CANWETAPE.pdf, accessed on 18 April 2015; or Association of American Physicians and Surgeons (2015) 'Summary of consent requirements for taping telephone conversations.' Available at www.aapsonline.org/judicial/telephone.htm, accessed on 14 March 2015; or Castillo, M. (2014) 'Was it legal to record and release Sterling's racist rant?' Available at http://edition.cnn.com/2014/04/30/us/nba-sterling-legality, accessed on 14 March 2015.

13. Czarnota, P. (2012) 'The right of publicity in New York and California: A critical analysis.' *Jeffrey S. Moorad Sports Law Journal 19*, 2. Available at http://digitalcommons.law.villanova.edu/mslj/vol19/iss2/3, accessed on 14 March 2015.

14. Mann, S. (2005) 'Sousveillance and Cyborglogs: A 30-year empirical voyage through ethical, legal, and policy issues.' *Presence Teleoperators and Virtual Enviornments 14*, 6, 625–646.

15. SHouse California Law Group (2014) 'California's "Peeping Tom" Laws.' Available at www.shouselaw.com/peeping-tom-laws.html#2.1.2, accessed on 18 December 2015.

16. See Rasmussen, K. (2011) 'Filming police in public is protected by the First Amendment.' Available at www.rcfp.org/browse-media-law-resources/news/filming-police-public-protected-first-amendment, accessed on 18 April 2015.

17. Hooton, C. (2014) 'The only person indicted over Eric Garner's death was the guy who filmed it.' Available at www.independent.co.uk/news/world/americas/the-only-person-indicted-over-eric-garners-

death-was-the-guy-who-filmed-it-9903797.html, accessed on 23 December 2014.

18. See the Crown Prosecution Service's 'Trespass and nuisance on land.' Available at www.cps.gov.uk/legal/s_to_u/trespass_and_nuisance_ on_land, accessed on 12 January 2015.

19. Strickland, P. (2014) 'Trespass to land.' Available at www.parliament. uk/business/publications/research/briefing-papers/SN05116/ trespass-to-land, accessed on 29 July 2015.

20. Poulter, S. (2011) 'Revealed: Shocking cruelty at massive abattoir...but those responsible WON'T be prosecuted.' Available at www.dailymail. co.uk/news/article-2020151/Abattoir-staffs-shocking-animal-cruelty-filmed-WONT-prosecuted.html, accessed on 17 January 2015.

21. The Canadian Press (2009) 'Duck poachers who posted YouTube video plead guilty in Saskatoon court.' Available at www.thetelegram.com/ Sports/Other-Sports/2009-08-10/article-170902/Duck-poachers-who-posted-YouTube-video-plead-guilty-in-Saskatoon-court/1, accessed on 30 July 2015.

UNDERCOVER TALES

Whistle-blowers: Threats and Fears

Most of the undercover cases in this book involve journalists or families, passers-by and citizens. This chapter deals with stories of a different group of people who are using hidden cameras and phone cameras. This is the story of employees; that is, where someone turns up at work and sees something that they don't like – sometimes something that they've complained about before – and occasionally they decide that they now have to film it. Sometimes those same people approach me. I hear from them usually only after they have exhausted every other avenue of complaint. The people I hear from often believe that instead of being taken seriously they have been ignored or marginalised. They come to me scared but feeling they have no other choice and so I make every reasonable effort to manage the risk to them from speaking out and to protect their identities if they wish. I always warn them about and help them mitigate any danger. That kind of care and worry is why even here I have anonymised these examples from my own experience of employees who have used cameras to record evidence.

Since 2012, three of the many care workers who have approached me did so after taking photographs – still images that appeared to show instances of poor care in their separate care homes. Each had already raised serious concerns about the care of vulnerable people. Sadly, each felt let down by the response they received and so decided they had to take photographs in order to prove what was happening. They felt that they had no choice left, faced as they were by sleeping colleagues or wet sheets and bent limbs, bruises and, in some examples, people left in a state of undress. (I'll come back to that last point in a moment.)

All of them were scared by the time they spoke to me, though. Some had even been told directly they would be in trouble for having their phone at work – that they would be sacked and could be questioned or even sued for invading the resident's privacy.

Although technically the property where they took the photos was not their own, they were allowed to be there as part of their work, and while they did not ask permission to take the photos, they were clearly well-motivated and concerned primarily, as far as I could tell, with the welfare of the elderly people in their care. It is not impossible that an employee of a care home could be sued for breach of privacy or trespass – again, I am no lawyer – but suffice to say that those care workers were not sued, and it would have seemed odd in my (non-lawyerly) view if they had been.

There is a wider ethical question which can affect the legal position of a worker who takes up cameras. One should be asking what absolutely needs to be recorded. In the context of care homes, for example, bruises, medical charts not filled out, broken windows, damp walls or specific misbehaviour can all be documented and so proven by a photo or other recordings. Those instances are worth recording – and are not too risky because they do not show people undressed. Ethical questions are mainly considered in Chapter 4, but ethical questions do affect the probability of legal questions. Even well-intentioned people can find themselves facing difficult questions, including from the authorities, if they carry around or, worse, show others photos or footage of vulnerable people undressed or naked. Workers particularly – because their position in relation to vulnerable people is much more precarious than first-degree relatives – should be careful about recording nudity, even if the intention is to try to protect that person. If in doubt, they should take legal advice.

There are other care workers I know who have also been fine, despite having filmed outright moving images or audio (not just taken photos) in order to protect the people in their charge.

Another senior care worker from a different institution approached me with footage and audio recordings that showed people mocking vulnerable adults, suggesting sexual acts they could perform with vibrators, simulating sex with a plastic bottle and sleeping when they should have been working – all captured with cameras in phones.

Those examples are rare, in my experience. I often hear about families buying and installing cameras to protect their loved ones, but I rarely hear about employees filming evidence. The reason, I suspect, is that employers are in a position of power over their employees.

It's a complicated situation when workers take up cameras at their place of business. There are a lot of questions they have to consider: Are they allowed to film things at work? Should they have a mobile or cellular phone on them? Did they make enough complaints and follow all the appropriate procedures before they decided to film something? Most places will have a whistle-blowing policy or rules about using phones. Were rules broken?

The fundamental and disappointing fact is that many employers – from any sector and type of business; public or private – often still do not like the people they pay raising concerns. That is true whether someone is producing footage of problems or just speaking out, that is, 'blowing the whistle'. One whistle-blower who I worked with said that not only did she feel that she suffered for speaking out about problems in a care home, she felt that her treatment prevented anyone else from raising issues or trying to do anything in future. 'I think the issues aren't dealt with enough and they're brushed aside, so why would anyone complain? Don't rock the boat. But you need to stick up for some people; otherwise, no one's gonna stick up for them,' she said. 'When I spoke out I expected things would really change but instead for years I felt shocked, numb, like "can this be real?", "is this another world I've walked into?"'

She felt worried for staff and residents at the care home where she had worked. How were they being treated? Had anything improved for them since she complained?[1]

Too often according to a range of charities and whistle-blowers, people raising concerns do not realise that they might need protection until it is too late. They see something wrong and speak out, because that is what they are supposed to do, right? A whistle-blower working with me at the moment – whom I cannot identify – says, 'I was so naïve, I always thought that they would do the right thing.'

There are two problems for employees who use cameras. The first problem is that they could be – and in some cases are – sacked. There is legislation in the UK that is supposed to protect whistle-blowers, but there are a number of loopholes and ways employers can get rid of someone that are still hard to fight. The second problem, though, is almost more difficult, because it is so hard to pin down. One might call it 'the fear'. Every legal discussion actually has two separate conversations buzzing around within it. The first conversation is about the stuff for which someone is actually likely to get sued. There is then a second discussion, a separate set of issues: how much hassle, legal threats and 'frighteners' will someone face?

After most of my investigations I have a pile of legal letters on my desk. Each one of those letters costs a fortune – money that could have been better spent tackling the issues I was highlighting. Too often the actual law as investigated by police officers or adjudicated by judges is not the real point for people blowing the whistle and/or for people using hidden cameras. I do not know anyone who has used secret cameras in the UK who has been sued for it or even arrested.[2] However, I know lots of people who have been threatened. Even when the law does not apply, threats are very effective. People are often easily frightened. For example, even where the laws of privacy and trespass do not apply, those laws are still quoted (or misquoted) to bully people. Families who have contacted me with secret footage from care homes have often had the frighteners put on them and have been cowed into silence. Members of the public, neighbours and families are really susceptible to such pressure. Employees are the group most susceptible to such threats. Employees who are working somewhere and who try to film things can too often be silenced.

People working in a number of institutions and sectors have said to me they wish something could be done about a range of social ills, but they would be too scared to carry a secret camera themselves.

Eileen Chubb, previously a whistle-blower and now a campaigner for better elderly care and for whistle-blowers in every sector, told me that she sees hidden cameras affecting workers who have concerns – sometimes in unpredictable ways.

She told me, 'I have seen other whistle-blowers accused of taking money from the media for the footage [when they secretly film something and allow it to be published]. That has come up quite a lot.'

The other complication she sees is that it is not just the 'good guys' doing the secret recording. She said, 'The other thing is there have been cases where [in care homes, for the vulnerable] the abuser has filmed the abuse, and their own footage has resulted in their conviction.'

Eileen believes that secret cameras can help whistle-blowers in future, if they use them sensibly and carefully.

'A whistle-blower using a camera can be accused by an employer of breaching confidentiality, but the bottom line is that cameras often result in prosecutions, while sadly on the flip side whistle-blowing on its own too often results in no action being taken. What matters is that the abuse [or other antisocial or illegal behaviour] is stopped,' she told me.

'My only regret as a whistleblower is that after reporting the abuse to management I did not use a camera.'[3]

The position for employees who want to carry out secret filming is complicated, not because the law is different per se (although, as stressed throughout this and the previous chapter, anyone with specific legal concerns should get independent legal advice) but rather because, if someone wants to speak out or wants to film something, it can be too easy for employers to frighten or bully their own employees. People can be driven out of their jobs if they complain, and the argument that we need to talk up the successes and encourage more people to speak out, an argument which I hear frequently, is really not that simple.

One whistle-blower, Dr Kim Holt, has spoken publicly about people saying the same thing to her: telling her to be positive. They tell her that she is back at work now, after all – surely that proves you can blow the whistle on major issues and still have a career. She spoke out about staffing levels and cultural issues in the community paediatric service part of Haringey's child protection system.[4] Her concerns were raised a year before a one-year-old child (Baby Peter Connolly, who died after severe physical abuse by his mother, her partner and her partner's brother and also after chances to save him were missed) was seen there.

So is hers a happy story for other whistle-blowers? Do they show that blowing the whistle can work out? Unfortunately, it is not that simple. Another whistle-blower, Ian Perkin, spoke out about financial misreporting by a hospital but says the current legal system provided him no meaningful protection. He said that even after the hospital trust admitted he was a whistle-blower, he still faced further allegations and a court battle which went on for years.[5] The current system did not link his whistle-blowing to the issues and accusations he faced after blowing the whistle. The law did not see the link. His employers argued they were just two different things: he happened to raise concerns and then just happened to have a series of concerns about his performance raised. He spent years and a vast amount of money fighting to try to clear his name, all the way through the British court system.

The Conservative blogger and writer Adrian Hilton wrote of his case:

> Ian Perkin...was employed as finance director of the St George's Healthcare NHS Trust in London. He had an impeccable record of service going back 33 years, with no complaints at all against him. Then, in

2001, he exposed poor practice in the cancellation of operations, and in 2002 he blew the whistle on the dire state Trust's financial affairs. All hell broke loose. His employers launched a counter-offensive disciplinary procedure, slandering and defaming him in the process. He was asked to resign, but refused. He was then subjected to an internal disciplinary process which determined (conveniently) that he should be dismissed. The reason was that he had 'an unreasonable management style' (though nobody had ever complained and no performance review had ever identified such a character flaw). Further, contrary to all principles of natural justice, he was denied an appeal against the decision.

It took many months for him to bring his case to an Employment Tribunal (with no job and no income). Astonishingly, although he was found to have been unfairly dismissed, the Tribunal judged that no compensation was payable because he had contributed 100% to his dismissal.

It beggars belief that a man with an unbroken and impeccable work record going back 33 years could, within a few months of blowing the whistle, suddenly be judged to have 'an unreasonable management style'. It is also quite incredible that no compensation was payable even though the St George's Healthcare NHS Trust had clearly harassed and bullied their employee (at the very least by not following their own procedures and denying natural justice).

Perkin appealed, and lost. He appealed to Government ministers and also to the former NHS chief executive Sir Nigel Crisp, but to no avail. He discovered, quite contrary to public statements and assurances, that 'the NHS offers no assistance at all to whistleblowers, and in fact you are completely on your own'.

Ever since the Perkin judgement, public bodies have been able to cling to the precedent that they can sack the whistleblower and take their chances in an Employment Tribunal. And the odds are on their side: the employee is undermined, defamed, destroyed, unemployed and unemployable. It will take a year (or more) for them to bring their case to Tribunal, with all the attendant worry and associated stress, and they are unlikely to be able to afford to wait for justice, which is invariably long-delayed, if it comes at all.

Further, the average compensation paid for unfair dismissal is only £8,000. If it is judged that your whistle-blowing contributed to your dismissal (which is highly likely), you may, like Perkin, end up with absolutely nothing. Effectively, you can now be dismissed on the grounds of personality, and you don't have a leg to stand on.[6]

Similarly, Dr Holt says that she was not helped by the law that is supposed to help whistle-blowers under the Public Interest Disclosure Act (PIDA) either – because she had not been sacked. Those worried about the protections currently on offer to whistle-blowers point out that until a complainant is actually kicked out of their job, and unless they have followed all internal procedures (which sometimes might say, for example, that a complainant has to go back to work alongside the people bullying them for speaking out), they get no protection from PIDA.

Great Ormond Street, her former employer, told the BBC in a statement that they saw the facts around her case differently:

We have said repeatedly that Dr Holt was unable to return to work in Haringey because of a breakdown in relationships between her and her colleagues in the service at the time. An NHS London report found that her concerns were taken seriously by the Trust.[7]

Dr Holt told me in an email:

My main argument about the law is that it does nothing to prevent the bullying that happens on a daily basis to so many health professionals who try to speak up. Staff surveys confirm the high level of bullying within the NHS.[8]

Dr Holt spoke out about problems in a local authority where child protection was failing abysmally, before a child died tragically and horribly. She said at a conference that after first complaining whistle-blowers:

...go through a shock period. They speak out in the NHS because it's part of their role, but then they get hostility or bullying, sometimes explicit such as being screamed at or shouted at – in one case a woman was shouted at until she collapsed unconscious – or more subtle making allegations against the person, behind the scenes.

It is in that context that people working in a range of industries are too scared to speak out – and equally scared to use hidden cameras. Instead, they are labelled as 'troublemakers'.

If there is one consistent message I hear from people working inside institutions that have problems, people who are trying to speak out or who have spoken out, it is that they wish they had sought help earlier, from people who could really support them. When such whistle-blowers take up cameras to gather proof, we need to recognise how vulnerable their position is and support them where possible for everyone's sake. Society needs good people to speak out about serious problems in every sector and any profession, if their concerns are not resolved through ordinary complaints and procedures. The future of secret filming and the willingness of people working in sectors across society to first speak out and then, where necessary, to gather evidence of wrongdoing is too important.

NOTES

1.   The care home owners in question denied that that ex-employee was a whistleblower, saying she was part of a group engaged in a dispute about pay and conditions. The previous owner said it had been a well-run home. The new owners told the BBC they put in place a range of improvements at the home.

2.   Police did arrest (then) BBC undercover reporter Mark Daly in 2003, but not for secret filming per se. They took him on suspicion of 'obtaining a pecuniary advantage by deception (his police wages), presenting false documents (he didn't let on that he had worked as an undercover reporter on his police trainee application form), and damaging police property (he made a hole in his bulletproof vest to hold a pinhole camera and battery pack)'. See Jeffries, S. (2003) 'Undercover cop.' Available at www.theguardian.com/media/2003/oct/21/bbc.raceintheuk, accessed on 21 March 2015.

3.   Eileen Chubb now runs Compassion in Care, www.compassionincare.com. For more information about her experience as a whistle-blower see: Anonymous (2000) 'Whistleblowers "forced to quit".' *The Guardian*, Friday 14 July 2000. Available at www.theguardian.com/uk/2000/jul/14/2, accessed on 12 September 2015; or Smith, A. (2014) '"There were hundreds of us crying out for help": the afterlife of the whistleblower.' *The Guardian*, Saturday 22 November 2014. Available at www.theguardian.com/society/2014/nov/22/there-

were-hundreds-of-us-crying-out-for-help-afterlife-of-whistleblower, accessed on 12 September 2015.

4. Haringey is a borough of London in the United Kingdom.

5. White, C. (2004) 'Whistleblower was unfairly dismissed, tribunal finds.' *British Medical Journal 328*, 7435, 310. Available at www.ncbi. nlm.nih.gov/pmc/articles/PMC1140671, accessed on 3 December 2015.

6. Hilton, A. (2013) 'Care Quality Commission cover-up: Whistle-blowing will seriously damage your health.' Available at http:// hiltonblog.dailymail.co.uk/2013/06/care-quality-commission-cover-up-whistle-blowing-will-seriously-damage-your-health.html, accessed on 25 April 2015.

7. BBC News (2011) 'Baby P whistleblower Dr Kim Holt says it is important to speak out.' Available at www.bbc.co.uk/news/uk-15522368, accessed on 1 May 2015.

8. See the website of Dr Holt's campaign group for more information about their views: www.curethenhs.co.uk/patients-first, accessed on 30 July 2015.

Chapter 6

WHAT YOU DON'T REALISE...

The Challenges That Most Often Surprise People

People embarking on secret filming and the people concerned by their activities should be warned in advance that there is a cost beyond the monetary price of the actual equipment. Those who take up cameras to oppose wrongdoing had better be ready to do a lot of unglamorous but essential tasks, and also they had better be prepared for the emotional issues involved. Invading someone's privacy with cameras and everything that entails *should* be tough. It is a big deal – difficult and often upsetting. Proper preparation for what is going to be involved can make a huge difference.

WHAT YOU MIGHT NOT REALISE IS REQUIRED TO DO SECRET FILMING WELL

Part 1: Additional logistical and physical considerations

MANAGING ANY SECRET FOOTAGE PROPERLY

All video footage recorded by a covert camera or mobile phone has to be downloaded to a computer. It should ideally also be backed up to a second drive (just in case one's computer crashes). That is time-consuming, but it is significantly better than losing evidence.

After that task has been completed, one needs to review all the footage that they have generated. There is no point to recording events that are not analysed. People who are using cameras have to watch the results and ideally keep notes with time codes and references to key events.

Even with just one operative wearing cameras for several 12-hour shifts a week, it takes me and someone else experienced in what to look for – and supported by experts and ethical advisors at the BBC – preposterous 15-hour days to really make sure we keep up in real time with what we are recording. It is absolutely worth it in the end. When anyone – professional or ordinary citizen – has interrogated their footage carefully and questioned every frame then their credibility is established, they are harder to challenge. The organisations someone is making accusations about and the range of professionals who will get involved (whether that be trading standards or the police, social workers or national regulators) should have more confidence that the person who filmed is one of the 'good guys' if they are 100 per cent clear about what they filmed. It is a pretty good first litmus test, and it is worth stressing because it is an area where even professional journalists sometimes try to skimp, as analysis of all the footage one has recorded is not a small task. That is probably the most onerous and problematic requirement for members of the public who are considering uncovering wrongdoing; however, it is essential.

Unless one watches everything carefully, one could have an incomplete picture of what is going on. That works both ways. One can miss evidence of wrongdoing or evidence of good behaviour. Both need to be considered, equally. For example, I worked with a family who had put a secret recorder in a care home, worried about how their relative was being treated. It was only when I watched but also transcribed every moment of the footage that I spotted a second distressed resident coming into the room briefly saying she couldn't find any care workers, that she did not know how to help their grandmother.

It's easy to think through secret filming to first base – getting a hidden camera and putting it somewhere – without realising what is going to be required to manage it properly. The logistical reality is that almost any secret filming will generate a significant amount of video and audio material. One has got to put in the necessary time to do it justice.

FOOTAGE IS NOT ENOUGH ON ITS OWN; PEOPLE NEED TO MAKE GOOD NOTES

Anyone doing secret filming must maintain good notes. This is not as onerous as backing up and watching everything someone records, but it is still another drain on the time of people doing filming. It is important, though: no one will be very impressed if a citizen journalist turns up with secret footage saying, 'I'm pretty sure I filmed that clip on the eighth because my brother's birthday was a few days after and I think it was a Saturday.' At the bare minimum, it should always be clear what day and what time covert recording began and then when it restarted, and so forth.

Making notes does not have to be a complicated process. One can use any lined notebook. It should be used only for that purpose – don't mix up filming notes with the shopping list. Just write the day's date at the top and put down enough to make clear what happened. For example, a note could be just: 'went in 8 a.m., got memory card out, replaced it with empty card, came home, viewed footage.' That sort of note removes all doubt. It proves what someone did and when. The advantage to it not being on the computer is that there is less room later for someone to argue the record was altered or fixed.

KEEPING THE CAMERA IN FOR LONGER

It would be understandable if one were to decide, faced with all these logistical demands, 'I'm only going to leave the cameras in for ten minutes!' I understand that impulse, so painful is the process. However, I would strongly counsel anyone doing serious filming to leave their camera in longer. Too often secret filming done by members of the public is just too brief. If someone only films a couple of times, it will mean they only film the same care worker or neighbour (or whoever) once or, at best, twice. That makes it too easy to claim, 'it's just a couple of bad apples' or 'it was a one-off'. It is very unlikely that one will be able to prove whether a set of problems are endemic in a care home after just two nights, for example. The test should be whether or not the cameras have proved there is a *pattern* of bad behaviour. So leave the camera in long enough.

That is counter-intuitive for many people. After many of the covert films I have made, the BBC was asked how we could leave a camera in, even after seeing something bad, sometimes even after seeing what could later be investigated as a crime. People ask why cameras were left in 'so long'. That question is upside down. They should usually be asking the opposite: 'Why weren't cameras left in longer?' If we need to secretly film in a given situation at all, then how can we walk away with just one example of wrongdoing? How can we simply say, 'We've seen one untoward thing' and stop, if (as should be the case; see Chapter 4 on ethics) we know that limited interventions and complaints have failed to change things in the past?

I should be clear that there are exceptions. Just as with the legal advice in Chapter 5, everything depends on the circumstances, and there could be circumstances where someone could be at immediate risk of substantial harm such as sexual abuse, permanent injury or death. Under such circumstances, obviously the right thing to do would be to immediately contact the authorities.

Part 2: The emotional cost of covert recording

Tamanna Rahman, a British-born journalist of Bangladeshi descent who went undercover on a predominantly white housing estate to expose racism,[1] told me:

> In my opinion, there are no glamorous bits – only glamorous-*sounding* bits. You can tell your friends or colleagues how you strapped on two cameras and caught someone being racist towards you or throwing a glass bottle at you. They listen open mouthed and impressed with your bravery. But really putting on a camera and simply 'being undercover' is very mundane. Most of the best bits of footage I caught were completely unexpected, and because of that,

despite being detached and aloof in general, they made me react quite unexpectedly emotionally.

There is a psychological cost to using hidden cameras: eventually the storm dies down, filming is finished and one is again back in their front room, thinking. After we are done secretly recording, most of us start to feel guilty – unreasonably and inappropriately guilty. Even where the people being secretly recorded have done terrible things, there is no getting around feeling guilty for having deceived them.

GUILT AND MEMBERS OF THE PUBLIC

I once assumed that these inappropriate feelings of guilt would only affect journalists, but that was wrong. It is even harder emotionally for *citizen* journalists. At least Tamanna and I had some distance by dint of it not being our 'real life'. We could go home to friends and family; we could put aside our 'second skin' even if only briefly. It is much harder when that is really *your* house and really *your* life.

I watched some of those guilt feelings up close when making films with families who had secretly filmed their own relative. They would not have described it as 'guilt', but I spotted it in them. For example, in one conversation someone would say they wanted to see prosecutions and punishment, and then, in the next conversation, they would say they hoped everyone working at the place they filmed would know they felt bad about the deceit involved with hiding a camera, and that they just wanted to improve things. Back and forth they would go, just like a yo-yo.

In the final analysis, any use of secret cameras always involves some level of deceit, even if sometimes it is justifiable. This sort of calculation – how much deceit is acceptable – affects all covert work.

The world's greatest undercover journalist, the German Günter Wallraff, has not primarily relied on filming in his investigations: he has experienced events and written them up in books and articles. Throughout those investigations, and using whatever means, Wallraff has pretended to be someone else. He has been taking on a false identity. In other words, his actions have involved a high level of deception.

Given the scale of the targets of his investigation and the amazing amount of social good he has achieved, there is no doubt Wallraff's work has been reasonable and proportionate. For example, he single-handedly probably prevented a right-wing coup in Portugal in the 1970s.[2] In the 1980s, he spent two years pretending to be a Turkish immigrant to expose the difficulties and realities of Germany's immigrant underworld.[3]

Günter Wallraff

For most members of the public who use secret cameras – or at least in all the examples I have come across so far – someone will not be taking on a false identity. The deception involved with their filming will be much more limited than in Wallraff's investigations, but someone should not pretend to themselves that it will be non-existent.

In the cases I know where a member of the public smuggled a camera into a care home, for example, they did need to explain at least why a 'new clock' or whatever else was turning up.[4] Most families I know who used hidden cameras ended up being questioned by someone, and unfortunately it was always the one person they liked, a care worker who was pretty decent. As a result, people I have worked with who used their own secret cameras had a terrible moment where they were making something up like 'Oh, I wanted to get (so-and-so) a birthday present' to tell to the one person they would rather not lie to.

If one has paid close attention to the ethical lessons in Chapter 4 and considered carefully what they are doing, then they will be in the right, and they will not have had a choice, but that won't stop them from feeling bad about it. It is just part of the emotional cost that has to be borne if one is going to try to change things by using hidden cameras.

Part 3: The solution (friends and family)

Given all the challenges set out above, I hope that people involved with secret filming will get support. Equally importantly, it would be great if the people affected by or concerned about covert recording realised what people using cameras go through and could offer them a bit more sympathy and understanding. I would strongly advise anyone against doing secret filming totally on their own.

It is not possible for one person alone to do everything required for covert filming of any duration.

Successful investigations carried out by journalists have involved teams of people. They are usually small – just big enough to cover the work, but tight-knit enough to maintain consistency. The same will be true in future: the best filming will be done by similar small groups of people but made up of affected family members, friends or volunteers. In short, nothing is more fundamental than the make-up of the team doing the filming.

It is a really big ask for the people who one recruits. For the amateur user of hidden cameras, it is much harder even than for teams of journalists. For example, at least I can pay people. By comparison, someone doing secret filming but looking for help may have to beg for assistance from people who usually work full-time and/or have other commitments. To make it work, secret filming needs to be logistically feasible at all times with as few participants as possible in order to maintain secrecy, but enough to cover the work involved.

Given the personal costs involved in secret filming, the next most important lesson for the new generation of citizen journalists and social activists doing it on their own is to look after the people helping them, because everyone is going to need support long after the filming is done and any wrongdoing has been exposed.

I do not know of any professional undercover journalist who cannot list a relationship, or often a number of relationships, that fell apart because of secret filming. Usually their partner felt both ignored and abandoned. Even worse, when someone who is doing secret filming is back at home, often their mind will still be on the filming, or it may even be damaged in some way. The film-maker often will still be spouting terrible truths – describing incidents the partner, husband or wife never signed up to have to hear. The same stresses apply to the families who have worked with me after doing their own secret filming.

It would be helpful if professionals and the people who support and are affected by secret filming could try to empathise with the emotional toll that covert recording can take. By its very nature, covert recording is incredibly taxing, and someone who has recorded anything secretly will almost always have sweated blood and fretted incessantly throughout the process.

The journalist Tamanna Rahman (see Chapter 5) told me of her time undercover:

> I was working pretty much 18-hour days. Even when not 'on duty' collecting evidence, there was the sifting through the footage, logging, doing a written diary, recording a video diary, doing drop-offs of memory cards and then the wait for the inevitable moment I had to go out again. It was a pretty relentless two months. I lost quite a bit of weight. I now think you should never trust a fat journalist!

People can change things for the better through secret filming, even if it hurts along the way.

NOTES

1. See Chapter 5 for more details on that BBC *Panorama* film, 'Undercover: Hate on the Doorstep.'
2. Wallraff, G. (1979) *The Undesirable Journalist*. New York, NY: The Overlook Press.
3. Wallraff, G. (1988) *Lowest of the Low*. London: Methuen Paperback.

4. It is possible to sneak some objects in unnoticed: there have been a few members of the public with whom I have worked who have come up with particularly cunning methodologies (which I won't divulge for fear of tipping off folks who may be scouring this book looking to 'catch someone out') to sneak stuff in.

UNDERCOVER TALES

Stories of Physical and Emotional Pain

I learned the physical costs of secret filming literally in marks on my thighs where I wore a camera too tight while working in a care home and in aching muscles after long physical shifts at a dozen different jobs. As for the emotional costs, I wept on the shoulder of girlfriends and colleagues.

PHYSICAL PAIN UNDERCOVER

One of my most extreme experiences working undercover wearing hidden cameras shows how using secret cameras can hurt physically. I was in the back of a large white van which was pounding along a motorway at 90 miles an hour with a gang of railway maintenance workers at 11 p.m. one night. It was the start of a shift. We were about to begin digging, all night long, again.

Tracy Chapman's song 'Fast Car' came on the radio. As I sat there in the dark, listening to this song, after two weeks shovelling heavy ballast in the dark and the rain on Britain's railways, I realised that, for that moment, I really did not know if it was worth it anymore. It's exactly the same mix of hope, danger and often weariness that families or other citizens experience when they use hidden cameras. Working on the train tracks and shovelling ballast while wearing big, old-fashioned, hard-to-hide cameras taxed me particularly worse physically than any other investigation where I wore secret cameras.

Each night, I slaved away until I was told to put down the shovel, exhausted. I would tramp back to the hotel to sleep all day. I would wake up in the afternoon disoriented and try to find somewhere to eat dinner when it felt as if it should be breakfast at 3 p.m. I would get my cameras back on at 7 p.m. having had just half an hour to call anyone or think about life outside the programme.

Then I would start all over again. Shovel, shovel, shovel. Film, film, film. Pouring rain, pitch black. Shovelling one night alongside a young African man, the two of us were just two railway maintenance workers, water streaming off as the sweat steamed up inside our plastic, heavy, orange waterproof coats. Dig, dig, dig. Collapse. Dig, dig, dig. I tried not to think about lots of things, tried to ignore the fact that these stones I was shifting were *designed* to be heavy – literally made not to shift easily under my shovel. I tried to ignore the giant modern machine parked next to us that could do the same job – get up the rocks and change the sleepers – in half the time. We were cheaper. So it stood, parked, inactive, and we dug.

'Pure Shawhank Redemption. Just Shawshank,' the guy shovelling next to me said – more to the rain and more to himself than to me – during one of our brief breaks. He was referring to the 1994 film classic *The Shawshank Redemption*, where prisoners were used in an illegal work scheme. This job he and I were doing was not illegally organised, but I know what he meant.

A guy can start to lose himself faced with such odds. I was completely spent. It was taking more out of me emotionally, physically and indeed socially (I had not seen friends or family for months) than someone outside the experience would imagine. Every early morning, back from working a night shift, at some hotel I was recording video diaries on a small tourist camera as well as writing up notes, backing up footage and reviewing what I had filmed.

It was not just the secret filming; it was doing the second job (as a journalist) as well. Such tasks, such difficult work and such personal costs often make secret filming an unenviable task. It certainly is not glamorous, and this is what people – the members of the public who are doing this sort of thing themselves and also the people concerned with or supporting their activities – need to realise. They will not be in such extreme circumstances (I hope), but many of the same essential challenges will arise when members of the public do their own filming.

In this case, because of all the sacrifice, I managed to get answers to a couple of basic questions about what's wrong with the railways in the UK, including answers related to over-expenditure and how accidents happen. One night, I asked a track worker (a guy just like me but with more experience) why we were just standing there, waiting to start work. No one had told me why. The answer was that our job had been planned for ages but somehow we had not been given possession of the track. A train might still whizz down it, so we couldn't start digging up ballast. This other railway maintenance worker (or 'shovel monkey' as the bosses sometimes called us to our face) was fed up. He had seen too much. He explained the truth about the sheer waste, incompetence and mismanagement of sub-contractors. The system simply was not working the way it should have worked.

'The one week we never even got out of the van. The next week I think we did about ten minutes [work],' he told me. 'This time it's just that they can't get this possession. Drives you barmy. They sent me up there the other week from way way over there – says go get three radios, I only thought it was about half a minute. It took me half an hour to walk up get three radios, and walk back trust me. It happens every week.'

There was always something – and we the tax payers were always paying men not to work even while our journeys were delayed.

The moral of the story for people using secret cameras is that the filming is often tough and drains more physical and emotional resources than one would expect, but if the filming is done well and for the right reasons, it can illuminate truths that make it worth the trouble.

EMOTIONAL PAIN UNDERCOVER

The odd thing I have learned first-hand about the guilt that deceit and betrayal engender with regard to hidden cameras is that it is essentially illogical and unpredictable. The times I have felt the most guilt – and been most wracked by its effects – are not the times I expected it. The emotion seems to tear one up the worst when it sneaks up on you. For example, certain times when I expected that secret filming would take a big toll on me emotionally and psychologically, to my surprise I coped perfectly well. There are other times where I thought an investigation I was carrying out would be straightforward, but then it struck me down emotionally – felled me where I stood.

One film that I worked on in regional BBC many years ago had one of the biggest emotional costs for me, and I really did not see the problems coming. I was investigating doorstep lenders. These are the companies that loan money from house to house mainly on poorer housing estates in Britain and many other countries. There has been much talk on the news in the UK about payday loans recently mainly because they are newer entrants to the market, but doorstep lenders have been targeting relatively poor people on estates around the UK for a much longer time.

The reason for both payday lenders and doorstep lenders is the same: high-street banks will not provide loans or credit cards to relatively poor people without a credit history and given their low earnings. Although Britain's credit unions have doubled their scale over the last decade, there remains a gap, so a market has sprung up supplying small loans to the poor. That in itself is no bad thing in theory, but some doorstep lenders (unlike credit unions) charge staggering interest rates, and there have been other complaints, such as those about the aggressive behaviour of some debt collectors. The industry has repeatedly denied these concerns, saying they are careful about how much they lend each customer and that they train and manage their staff carefully.

We wanted to see for ourselves. Working with (then) producer Andy Head, we had spoken to a range of people who said to us that they had not only been charged high interest rates but also that they had suffered a range of shady tricks – unethical and in some cases illegal mechanisms for charging them more money, running up more debt and sometimes even threatening them.

I would not be undercover for that long – a matter of days, rather than the weeks that I had sometimes spent wearing hidden cameras. All in all, it seemed emotionally and physically less draining than most of the things I had done undercover. But it didn't work out that way.

I got work with a door-to-door debt seller and was assigned to shadow a woman I will call 'Susan', a collector for a major provider of doorstep loans. Susan laughed as she explained the situation. 'We're loan sharks,' she said when I first sat down in the office.

We came out and got in her car. She set off to show me how rounds are completed, interest collected and loans handed out. Susan was blunt as we travelled, explaining exactly how the business works: 'Our interest rates…well, they're eye-opening.'

At that time with that company, someone would pay back £150 on a £100 loan. As I went around the doorsteps, people did not seem to realise that. All they knew was that they would pay back £5 a week. They certainly were not told there were cheaper options. No one we spoke to seemed to have checked if they could get a bank account or go to a credit union.

Then there were all the other tricks I saw her use. For example, I saw Susan convince people to take out a new loan if they were struggling to pay the interest on old loans. That meant in effect they would pay interest on the interest they were already being charged, at the same eye-popping rates.

At the top of one of Brighton's housing estate towers, giant white stacks with balconies around every edge, I watched Susan ask a 12-year-old, 'You'll take a loan when you're 18, right?' Furthermore, she was already at the point where she was collecting money from women who she had known as children. It struck me from watching her interactions that in a way Susan – not just her customers – was a victim of the company too. The company was, even if unconsciously or unintentionally, using *her* to access an entire community to charge high interest on small loans.

'If we can get your payments up, then you'd be down to £50 by Christmas and I could loan you more. We want to keep your debt down, don't we? To make some room for Christmas?' she said to a client, convincing them – in a way that I will never fathom, but which worked somehow – to borrow more money so that they could get more loans to keep up their payments.

'We haven't had a payment in a while…Christmas is coming, if we can't get a payment now, I won't be able to help you out then,' she said to one client.

'You're nearly paid off…you're not going to leave me without a loan, are you? You'll take out another £100 right?' she said to another.

'Do you know your mother's mobile number?' she said, extracting information from a minor without their parents' permission. A knowing gleam in her eye, it seemed to me she knew she was trying her luck – but it worked: she got the number and now could chase the loans over the phone, not just in person.

I filmed all of these interactions on a secret camera, for a programme for regional BBC.

Shopacheck, Susan's company, refused to be interviewed for the programme but issued the following statement:

> Shopacheck is a responsible lender and cares about its customers and representatives. Shopacheck is licensed under the Consumer Credit Act and conducts all its operations in accordance with its regulatory requirements.
>
> The BBC refused to show us the footage prior to screening meaning we were unable to comment.

> We will of course take all criticisms seriously and
> investigate them thoroughly.[1]

I went in with a clear conscience, feeling keen to expose the system. I am proud of the film that we made at regional BBC. That film locally helped the credit union, and throughout the UK it became part of the National Consumer Council's super complaint into the behaviour of doorstep lenders.

There was another less positive outcome, though, for me: I ended up on my (then) producer's doorstep late at night in tears. The reason was that the woman I've called 'Susan' here was – as I've outlined above – a victim too. She is and was a real person with a real-life husband, a real-life life. What she did was wrong, but I now knew her, too well really. Even though the film could not have been more worthwhile, secret filming always involves deception and great difficulties, and pain is often one of the results.

That producer, Andrew Head, summed up the problem in that case bluntly when we talked about this again recently: 'As an undercover operative it is your job to get close to people. You befriend them and then betray them. Even though they may be up to no good, that is hard on a personal level.'

NOTES

1.   BBC (2004) 'Financing debt.' Available at www.bbc.co.uk/insideout/south/series5/debt_finance.shtml, accessed on 1 May 2015.

Chapter 7

WHAT DO YOU DO WITH IT?

What Happens After the Camera Is Switched Off

Mandy Mugford secretly filmed her mother's pain (or fear of pain) and clear distress in a care home for the elderly. She told me:

> My mum suffered and I cannot do anything to make that go away. That is going to be in my head for evermore. It's in my heart. My dear mum suffered at the hands of negligent people. I don't want that to ever, ever happen to another living soul. I know I can't do anything about mum, but I sure as hell am not going to sit back and not try to help others. It mustn't be allowed to carry on.

Her decision to use hidden cameras and what she filmed are discussed in the 'Undercover Tales' at the end of this chapter, but there is a story after she was done secretly filming: it is the story of what happens after someone has switched off their hidden camera for the last time.

This chapter discusses what happens when the cards are put on the table, when everything is out in the open. Switching off a hidden camera is not the end of the journey; it just opens up a whole new set of questions which people have to answer. We all could be better prepared for what happens after secret recording finishes.

THE STEPS TO TAKE AFTER THE CAMERA IS SWITCHED OFF

Step 1: Declaring there is footage, usually in a hurry

Members of the public with whom I have worked stopped their secret filming when they saw something they found intolerable. For example, a 'bad guy' may have hit someone, and now they have to tell the authorities this minute. As a result, members of the public who have done secret filming are often declaring their evidence urgently to get instant resolution: they want someone sacked or something changed *now*.

Most investigations – and indeed prosecutions – involved with secret footage actually take a while. Dropping a huge bundle of information on a company or organisation can mean that right from the word 'go' there is a disconnect between the people filming and the people receiving the footage. People who want instant action need to prioritise their material and the reaction they are seeking so that the most important issues are resolved first. If someone doing secret filming has been carefully reviewing their footage as they go along, they should have good notes and should be able to prioritise the most immediate major concerns first, and present the 'smaller-ticket items' (i.e. the less urgent problems) later. They can help professionals and the people filmed to react better.

Being clear and concise about what needs to be done gives the people affected by or interested in the secret filming the best chance of responding appropriately. That is important because the moment someone declares that they have footage, it is a shock for the recipients. That is the first moment that the recipient(s) discovers that filming has been going on. All the worry, consideration, planning, setting up and recording that someone has done until now has been in secret.

Too few people respond appropriately, at least at first. I have seen secret footage dismissed, and I have seen companies attempt to manipulate the people who filmed it. It is usually most appropriate for professionals, such as social workers and inspectors, to thank people for unmasking wrongdoing and then get on with sorting out the problems they have exposed. If someone who used a secret camera first considered carefully why they were filming, and did it well, then they should be told, 'Well done!' and 'Don't feel guilty.' Instead, people who turn up with covert recordings sometimes get pummelled with questions like, 'Why did you do it?' or 'Why didn't you tell someone sooner?' or 'How do you know what it really shows?' or 'Why didn't you tell me first?' or – and this is sadly a genuine example from an organisation that had ignored complaints until an employee finally filmed evidence on their phone – 'You're not supposed to have your phone on shift. Do you realise that you could get in trouble?'

Maybe some of those questions – which don't help matters and often start arguments – could be avoided or at least postponed until a later date; if not, people doing secret filming certainly can be better prepared for them. Just like the Victorian heroine and undercover journalist 'Nellie Bly' was put in front of a grand jury and challenged over her revelations about the treatment of people in a psychiatric institution (see Chapter 4, 'Undercover Tales'), people who do secret filming need to be ready to be questioned and challenged.

Step 2: Addressing the question 'Can I have a copy of the raw footage?'

Every member of the public that I have met who has done their own secret filming has been asked by someone, usually the owner of the company where they filmed secretly, 'Can I have a copy of *all* the raw footage?' or even told, 'I *need* a copy of everything you filmed.' That is a more stark choice than it could appear at first glance. Should someone hand over all their filming to the people they are worried about, to the organisation they filmed? Do they just show clips? Do they make the footage public first?

The film-maker will have to make up his or her own mind, but I feel bound to offer a word of warning. Handing over the totality of the footage that has been recorded does not always work out well. A company can use having a copy of the footage to try to undermine the evidence, to ignore the substance and look for tiny ways to criticise or question the person doing the filming.

There are examples I know where based on simply viewing – not taking away or keeping – the footage, companies have conducted investigations and reviews. It is quite possible to learn what needs to be learned without the company or organisation taking possession of the footage. There are other examples where companies have taken secret footage and got lawyers to analyse it, looking for anything that they could find to undermine it and question its veracity.

Step 3: Deciding whether to go to the media

There is another calculation one has to make. Does one approach the media? Does one want their problems exposed to the whole world? Obviously, people who record secret footage do not have to take it to a journalist. Many people who make secret recordings do not actually publish their material. However, if the evidence they have captured is serious and shows really bad things, then some people do feel that there needs to be wider exposure. They want lessons to be learned.

People who approach me have often been worrying about the wrong issues – before they actually talk to me. For example, they often are worried whether I would misrepresent or 'sensationalise' their footage. I understand the worry because some journalists might do that kind of thing, but I don't. On the flip side, many people I meet have *not* been worrying about the most important potential problems, like what the reaction at the school gate will be when they next take their child into class after a film about any subject involving them is broadcast – where it involves intimate, and so in some ways embarrassing, personal information. Obviously, no matter how carefully I craft a film, I can't control what people who view my TV programmes say or do after a programme has been broadcast. I've seen people almost wilfully misinterpret some films – perversely turning the meaning upside down and backwards.

Opening yourself up to public scrutiny can help change issues that concern you, but it also means that you have to be prepared for every possible flavour of reaction – the good, the bad and the ugly.

'WHY NOT JUST PUT IT UP ON YOUTUBE OR FACEBOOK?'

I get this question sometimes. I was giving a talk once in a private Hampstead school when one 17-year-old at the back of a set of bleachers asked, 'Won't people in future just post anything instantly on YouTube or Facebook?'

Are gatekeepers like me actually just slowing people down? Will the future be people not just recording footage themselves but also broadcasting it on their own?

Most people who record their own footage need good advice about the upsides and downsides to publication. I can assist someone who has recorded their own footage in two ways. First, I have been able to protect and help the people who appeared in my films. Second, and sometimes more importantly, I can draw out the wider meaning of what they recorded, which increases its impact. If someone stuck footage of mistreatment in a care home on YouTube, it might garner a number of hits and maybe even some news coverage, but it would likely generate relatively little analysis or political impact. Many of the citizen journalists and families I have known have been criticising major organisations, large companies with sometimes unsympathetic professionals. In those circumstances, they really need more than just a website where they can upload their filming.

If someone decides after reflection that they want to explore whether or not to publish their footage, then it is easy enough just to email me at the BBC's *Panorama* programme. However, someone might instead decide they wish to call a lot of news outlets about their footage. Thomas Harding suggested the following to would-be 'video activists' (the readership he was addressing in his book) who wanted to get their recordings out there:[1]

> As your aim is to get the footage seen by as many people as possible you may as well try and sell the footage to as many broadcasters possible...don't underestimate the power of local and regional television. For example, BBC Newsroom South East has a reach of over 10 million people... Call the main number of the station and ask for the newsdesk. If it's the BBC you'll have to say which newsdesk: 1 o'clock, 6 o'clock, etc. When you get through, say that you're an independent video-maker and that you have some footage for the next news broadcast, then ask who you should talk to. You probably won't get the right person straight away but will be transferred one or more times, so don't give your best effort until you know you've got the right person. The conversation might go something like this:

> VIDEO ACTIVIST: Hello, my name is Jill Parsons and I've got some really exciting footage for your next news broadcast.

> JOURNALIST: What is it about?

VIDEO ACTIVIST: Well, I've just come back from a rally
                    outside the Houses of Parliament
                    where the Lesbian Avengers
                    handcuffed themselves to each other
                    to pressure the government to lower
                    the age of consent. There were over
                    thirty people.

Harding's advice is very useful, but it does presume that everyone wants to put their footage out through as many different avenues as possible, all at once. It ignores the potential to make longer films, like the ones I make on *Panorama*, which require more work but can go into greater depth. That does not rule out news coverage as well; it just delays it until the longer film goes out. It is a tactical decision. I have always made films for long-form television rather than news because I would rather work a little longer and dig a little deeper, rather than quickly get something out. Anyone doing covert filming will have to decide which approach to take if they want to get their footage out into the media. In the UK, there are programmes like *Panorama* or *Newsnight* (also on the BBC) and *Dispatches* (at Channel 4) which will do longer investigations. There are similar TV programmes in other countries. Journalists can usually only do those longer films with exclusive footage. They need to be able to justify the additional time and expense involved – and that means that the recordings need to have not been given to anyone else.

Step 4: Being patient after going public

After someone has finished secretly filming, declared what they have found and decided whether or not to work with journalists, any number of things could happen. The results depend very much on what someone has filmed and whether criminal charges may flow from the evidence. For example, there might be police prosecutions based on footage. In those cases, the people involved with recording secret footage need to brace themselves for a long journey, as the trial process in the UK, as elsewhere, can take months or even years. Other types of internal or public inquiries also may take a long time.

The point is that when someone records anything covertly, they need to know in advance – and brace themselves for the fact – that almost any official reaction is likely to take time. They need to be ready for a marathon, not a sprint, and must learn to live with the frustration. All the possible reactions to secret footage – court cases, inquiries, reviews and investigations – take a lot of time and effort to be completed.

COURT

My experience is that the court cases that sometimes follow secret filming are extremely tough – particularly if someone has to give evidence against the people who were filmed. I have done many difficult things in my life and been in stressful or dangerous circumstances again and again, but taking the witness stand in an adversarial court system just about tops it all.

A year and a half after I had worked undercover at an animal sanctuary in order to expose the mistreatment of birds, I stood in the witness box. The sanctuary's owner sat in the back of the courtroom. I avoided meeting his eyes while I was giving evidence.

INQUIRIES

A lot of secret footage does not produce criminal charges, but there can still be inquiries or reviews. Care homes, nurseries, animal sanctuaries, abattoirs, offices and companies that have been secretly filmed will often investigate the allegations that appear in any footage. In the best cases that is a genuine attempt to learn lessons and ensure mistakes are not repeated. Sometimes, however, it can be an attempt to play for time, an excuse to try to say, 'We cannot comment while we are carrying out an inquiry.' Those inquiries usually need the person who has recorded footage to answer yet more questions and do more work. They also involve more waiting – for answers *and* results. That can be upsetting for someone who usually just wants results and wants change after everything they have been through.

The truth is that the aftermath of secret filming is often very slow and can too often require chivvying and continued pressure. Events don't cease just because someone has switched off the camera. It is not all over.

Step 5: What happens after the circus leaves town (that is, once it is all finished)

I started this chapter talking about Mandy Mugford, whose experience illustrates one of the main truths about secret filming – a truth that does not become apparent to most people who do their own secret filming until after the camera is switched off. Mandy filmed poor care and pain (or the fear of pain) in one room in one care home, but she suspected that the same sorts of problems were continuing elsewhere. Although a few care workers were taken to task over her secret footage, she feared that the wider care sector and some bosses were not learning the lessons that would prevent other people's mothers and loved ones from suffering the same sort of experiences. To drive through social change would take more than once having done secret filming. Mandy decided that it would take campaigning long after the camera finished recording and after everyone else – all the inquirers, film-makers and social workers – had packed up and left. For Mandy, it still wasn't done.

Mandy has done everything she can think of to turn that loss and suffering into action. She has set up a website memorial to her mother and is trying to raise awareness about what can happen in care homes and nursing homes. Last time we emailed, she said she was writing a book. As part of the film she made with me for the BBC's *Panorama* programme, we filmed with her as she went to two shopping malls in Trowbridge collecting signatures for a petition. She said:

> It was amazing, the number of people that approached us. It was just outstanding, the results we got: over 700 signatures and I think that we were only out for three hours, and Trowbridge isn't exactly a huge town, so if we can get that many results in Trowbridge in a short space of time, then I can only imagine what we would get in bigger towns.
>
> I spoke to so many people on Saturday that were saying the same things to me that I felt when mum was in that nursing home, and they've lost their loved ones and some of them have still got loved ones in

>   nursing homes or residential homes and it's not just
>   nursing homes or residential, it's home care.

Just as Mandy discovered, there is a time after it is all done when you are no longer at the epicentre of events – that is, reviewing footage, proving things, deciding whether to broadcast it and possibly involved with a police investigation. Then, suddenly, people find themselves thinking, *Now what? What do I do next?*

When have they done enough? What *is* enough? Secret filming is never the end in itself, and no matter how powerful the footage, there will always be problems that remain. So how does one carry on and just walk to the shops and in the park, watch television and go to the bar day after day now that you know what is going on behind closed doors? Most people don't. Now that their eyes have been opened, they find themselves thinking, *What else can I do?*

Most of the people I know who used hidden cameras ended up as committed social activists, campaigners by another name. It is hard to turn a blind eye, and no major social ill ends just after one film or one piece of footage. Secret filming is both a blessing and a curse. It allows someone to make things better but burdens them with an insatiable duty.

One songwriter, Adelline Daley, contacted me when one of my films was broadcast to say she had blown the whistle on adults being mistreated in a care home. She told me that although she had not used hidden cameras, the experience had left her determined to change things in other care homes. She arranged for the singer Chantel Baylee to record a song that she wrote, and now 'Behind Closed Doors' is available online. The lyrics of the song include: *I saw it in her eyes, the suffering and the pain she was in.*

She was all alone. Isolated by this home where they drag old souls across the floors all behind those care home doors.

Adelline, Mandy and others, having seen how some of the most vulnerable people in society are treated, cannot look the other way. With a searing honesty, people like them are carrying on and trying to find ways to improve things. For them, it is no longer about just using secret cameras.

NOTE

1.   Harding, T. (2001) *The Video Activist Handbook* (2nd ed.) (p.108). London: Pluto Press.

UNDERCOVER TALES

Secret Filming in Care Homes

Care is the frontline for people doing their own secret filming at the moment in the UK. It is where covert recording is happening most right now. England's national regulator for health and social care, the Care Quality Commission (CQC), decided as a result that they even needed to offer guidance on using cameras in care homes.[1] Filming has become central to the discussion of social care in the UK. That fact is controversial. There are particular concerns about privacy in care homes and other health settings.

Andrea Sutcliffe, chief inspector of adult social care at the CQC, said:

> There have been a wide range of views on this subject, from those who think that cameras should have been installed years ago, to those who think I am the devil incarnate for suggesting it. We have decided that the best way to proceed is to issue guidance so providers and relatives who feel the need to do it know what the issues are that they need to take into account. Respecting the dignity of people is central.[2]

What happens within the care sector's doors is a bellwether for the morality of any country. The way a society cares for the elderly or the disabled, the ill and children is the clearest measure of that society's overall regard for its citizens.

This section includes two stories about when hidden cameras were used in Britain's elderly care homes: my experience and the experience of one family.

When I worked in an elderly care home undercover in my twenties, I witnessed poor care and mistreatment of people who had in some cases literally fought tyranny, people who were heroes and survivors of the Second World War.

One resident I will call 'Sarah' would frequently weep and complain, so she was labelled 'trouble'. At the end of one shift, as I sat next to two care workers waiting to leave, I watched my colleagues as they watched Sarah. They were laughing because she could not get into the building by herself in her wheelchair. They enjoyed watching her weakness and her struggle. On a different day, I walked along a hallway with two other care workers, including the most senior care worker in the home, one of the three senior care workers who effectively ran the place. A third care worker was sitting in an easy chair in the hallway. Sarah was lying in bed sobbing just opposite where the care worker was sitting. Sarah was raising her arm out, asking the care worker to help her out of her room. The care worker did not budge. The two care workers I was with asked the third one sitting down what was going on. The care worker explained that Sarah wanted to get out of her room to see the sun. The care workers wanted to change her pads and leave her in her bed, because dinner was coming up. During the discussion that ensued, according to this care worker, Sarah had called her a bitch. So now the care worker was sitting outside watching Sarah beg and apologise. The other two started joking, egging each other on. They told each other she was a pain and should just be left. They got worse – building up until they were shaking their fists at her, shouting threats.

Entering that nursing home was like crossing into a different universe. Outside there were quiet suburban streets, a little shop on the corner and blistering summer sunshine. Inside there was a netherworld of constant grey light and a regime and culture that turned according to its own logic. The home ran according to the needs of the *workers*. Some of them were very nice to the residents, but there were many who were not nice.

Without our secret filming, none of that would have been exposed. These types of problems had been picked up by the national regulator previously, but the problems had continued. The home had lost many good staff, and the people living there still lacked basic care. Even worse, like Sarah, sometimes they were being mistreated or threatened.

There was another resident – I'll call him 'Samuel' – whose poor treatment upset me even more. Samuel had served in Africa during the Second World War. He had moved into a nursing home after a stroke left one side of his body paralysed. One morning I found that his urine had saturated his pad and soaked the bed. A good care worker said he suspected that Samuel had been left like that by the night staff. (He could only guess, from the quantity of urine that had soaked past the pad.) This care worker was disgusted. He said, 'I wouldn't want *my* dad left like this.'

Samuel could not dress himself, and on another morning, I helped him into his trousers. He pointed out that the zip was broken. He was worried his penis would be exposed. I went to his drawer and pulled out his blue trousers: the zip on them was broken as well. Samuel told me he had complained about this before. All his trousers had broken zips.

I got Samuel dressed as best I could and then found a care worker. This one wasn't interested. She told me to ignore it. She said Samuel was 'trying it on' because I was new.

Sitting in his seven-by-ten-foot room, usually perched in his chair (unless someone wheeled him to the communal rooms for meals) – the TV blasting at whatever pitch the care staff had left it – Samuel somehow maintained his sense of dignity, even as his trousers were left unfixed.

Just two days later, I was again told that Samuel's pad clearly had not been changed by the night staff. (Another care worker said it could be that night staff just could not be bothered or it could be that they had been short-staffed.) Twice in three days he'd been left in his urine by night staff.

At the time, I wrote the following, under a pseudonym, for *The Guardian* newspaper:

> The owners of the care home were informed of our investigation. They were told specifically that we had seen care staff ignore residents' call bells, that some staff had been disrespectful towards residents and their needs, and that there were concerns about the level of hygiene and care that was provided. We detailed specific instances that would be shown in our film.[3]

A spokesperson responded to our concerns by stating:

> We pride ourselves in providing a high standard of care, so we are extremely concerned with the points we understand may be raised in the programme. We notified the National Care Standards Commission as soon as Five [a UK television channel] made us aware of their undercover probe. We also launched an

immediate internal inquiry which is still progressing, and any shortcomings identified will be speedily addressed.[4]

We'd had no choice but to employ secret cameras. I am proud that we tried to do something to highlight and hopefully stop what was going on, to help those people maintain their dignity.

———————————

Filming by families and carers remains controversial, and is being contested – some people want it banned. In June 2015, the Royal College of Nursing's conference in Bournemouth passed a resolution to oppose covert surveillance. Seventy-five per cent voted in favour.

There was no genuine debate, and contentious claims were not opposed. For example, Dr Peter Carter, Chief Executive of the RCN, said, 'If you have a care assistant who is unkind, uncaring and has entirely the wrong attitude, I don't think a camera is going to stop them. It may stop the overt stuff, but it won't stop the attitudinal stuff, or the cutting corners.'[5]

I've made five films about social care over a three-year period, which were broadcast on national television. Each of those films featured secret footage, filmed by either ourselves or families, which highlighted – and in some cases led to prosecutions targeting – unkindness, uncaring attitudes, cutting corners and neglect. There are real families out there, facing serious concerns, who feel that no one is listening to their worries. Nurses have genuine concerns, but they are ill-served by debate such as the one that took place in Bournemouth in June 2015.

ONE FAMILY'S EXPERIENCE

Mandy Mugford was not a professional journalist or television film-maker. She was a member of the public, a daughter concerned about her mother's treatment in a nursing home. Mandy felt her mother, Margaret Heslop, deserved better treatment than she was getting. Margaret had served her country during the Second World War, growing food in the land army.

'Where I grew up, all the children in the area called her "Nan". My friends would call her "Mum". Mum was just there for everybody,' Mandy said.

Margaret (Mandy's mum)
Source: Copyright © Mandy Mugford

By 2012, Margaret needed help with almost everything from getting her dentures in to dressing and having a drink of water. She had become terribly thin. Mandy always wanted to care for her mother herself, at home, but Margaret wanted to be around people her own age. Margaret wanted to move into a care home to make friends. So Mandy found one nearby that seemed good and helped her mother get settled there.

Instead of Margaret receiving the help she needed at that care home, she was left bedridden, unable even to sit up. Mandy believes this deterioration was caused by poor care. Mandy finally moved her mother to a second nursing home where they promised Margaret's retracted legs and mobility would be handled appropriately. For a little while it looked hopeful at that second care home. Some staff at the home said they were determined to get Margaret sitting up again. Mandy recalled:

> One nurse did get mum out of the bed and into a chair within 23 hours, and we were absolutely elated. She took a photograph and left it in mum's room for me to see. It was the first time mum had sat in a chair in about eight months.

The good news did not last. When some particularly good care workers were not there, Margaret would just lie in her bed, her knees pressing into each other and her hip bending, her bed squeezed between a plastic-texture chair and a cheap wardrobe. She would cry out in pain, or the fear of pain, when she was moved, sometimes apparently because her knee wasn't being supported. Mandy started to worry that the care home and too many of its workers seemed to have become inured to her mother's discomfort, to assume that Margaret's crying out in pain was just something she did. Mandy believed her mother's leg was swinging wildly, pulling her hip and hurting her frail joints. At other times, she believed Margaret had started to cry out because she feared being hurt.

Mandy sat in the unoccupied bedroom next door when her mother was being dressed. She would wince as she heard her mother screaming again and again, day after day. Mandy could not bear to hear her mother in such discomfort.

Margaret Heslop
Source: Copyright © Mandy Mugford

Mandy herself had worked in care homes for elderly people. She knew it did not have to be like this. Even without hidden cameras, many homes that have problems could start by just listening to the concerns of the relatives of their residents. Relatives may not always have the answer, but sometimes they may have spotted the problem. Mandy said:

> Nurses and other care home staff have to learn to listen to what families are saying, particularly when the person can't say it for themselves. Very occasionally, a family might not be getting it right, but nine times out of ten, from my experience, the family are saying things that need to be listened to, and what is ten times worse is that most of the time they shouldn't be the ones that are having to point it out in the first place.

Mandy did not feel that care workers at the home were taking her concerns seriously. She did not know what to do to help her mother. She started thinking about hidden cameras. She had seen one of the films that I produced in which the daughter of a care home resident hid a secret camera in her mother's bedroom in a care home. Mandy thought to herself that maybe if she showed the bosses of the care home how their staff were treating her mother, maybe if she hid a miniature camera without the staff knowing, then she could change things. It was a scary decision to have to make. Would she get in trouble? Mandy's daughter, Stacey, was not keen on the idea:

> When my mum first asked for us to look into cameras to go into my nan's room, I talked her out of it because I was concerned by doing so that she could get prosecuted or into a lot of trouble for recording people without them being aware of this. So she put it off.

Mandy waited, hoping things would improve. Finally, she felt she had no choice. Mandy said:

> I went in to see Mum and her little knees were digging into each other, bone on bone – dents in her skin...I mean, she was skin and bone. They weren't looking after her leg and stopping her leg from flopping around and hurting her hip and her knees.

Mandy did put in a secret camera. That hidden lens connected to a digital recorder proved care workers were ignoring her mother's pain or fear of pain, again and again leaving her to cry out – once even accusing her of feigning pain, saying, 'You have no tears.' Mandy said:

You could see Mum was afraid – she was afraid of the care workers. I just find it so hard to comprehend that we weren't quicker to pick things up, why it had to go as far as it did before we hid the camera. Mum should never have gone through that. Mum was such a beautiful person. To think that people were treating her badly...people were manhandling her. I can't bear the thought of anybody else going through what my mum went through.

Five care staff were sacked and six disciplined as a result of Mandy's footage. A BBC *Panorama* film in June 2013 showed the footage to the world.[6] If she had not hidden a camera in her mother's room, none of that would have happened. Mandy's mother's pain or fear of pain might have continued. Mandy said:

Those...I don't know what to call them...treated her like that. That was just one room; only one room in that nursing home had that camera in it and 11 people were suspended because of what we've seen. What went on in all the other rooms? I can cry for my mum but I'm crying inside for all the other people in all the other nursing homes and care homes, and not just that but home care as well. It needs to stop. They need to stop it happening to all these people.

Mandy knows how hard care work can be – as above, she used to be a care worker. She still thinks the home could have listened to her concerns – before she put in a camera. If they had listened, there might have been no need to secretly film anyone.

The care home where Mandy secretly filmed her mother told us at the time when we made the film that most of its staff do a demanding job very well, and that when they don't do so the owners and managers takes prompt action.

In almost every setting where I see secret cameras used, whether it is in care homes or nurseries, hospitals or animal sanctuaries, neighbourhoods where racist neighbours are victimising people or landlords or debt collectors are terrorising folk, the problems could have been avoided. There were warnings that were ignored, people who could have been listened to.

The debate about secret filming in care homes, hospitals and nursing homes no doubt will continue to rage. People more concerned about privacy will do battle with people who want in every room. However, that debate detracts from the most important truth about secret filming and social care: if excellent care were provided for all people in care homes, secret filming would never be necessary.

NOTES

1. Care Quality Commission (2015) 'Using hidden cameras to monitor care.' Available at www.cqc.org.uk/content/using-hidden-cameras-monitor-care, accessed on 31 July 2015.

2. Davies, E. (2014) 'Families given official green light to spy on care home staff if they fear their elderly relatives are being abused.' Available at www.dailymail.co.uk/news/article-2781719/Watchdog-help-record-relatives-carers-catch-abuse-Care-Quality-Commission-issue-guide-using-CCTV-month.html, accessed on 7 October 2014.

3. Lyon, R. (2003) 'Neglect on the home front.' Available at www. theguardian.com/society/2003/dec/17/longtermcare, accessed on 2 May 2015.

4. Borland, S. and Sinmaz, E. (2015) '"Ban worried relatives from filming the elderly in care homes," argue nurses who "don't want to be scrutinised".' *Daily Mail*, 22 June 2015. Available at www. dailymail.co.uk/health/article-3134928/Ban-worried-relatives-filming-elderly-care-homes-argue-nurses-don-t-want-scrutinised.html, accessed on 4 July 2015.

5.   BBC (2013) *Panorama: Elderly Care: Condition Critical?* BBC1, 17 June. See www.bbc.co.uk/programmes/b02zg3h2, accessed on 31 July 2015.

Chapter 8

WHERE DO WE GO FROM HERE?

The Next Generation of Covert Cameras and the Future of Secret Filming

Secret filming will affect more lives and advance into more sectors in future, assuming it isn't banned.[1] There are three reasons that secret cameras are bound to increase their reach in years to come. The first reason is that cameras (both in mobile or cellular phones and 'proper' secret cameras) are getting cheaper. As better-quality cameras become more affordable, more people will use them to record serious evidence. Second, new types of cameras are coming online, particularly flying and remote cameras. Finally, secret cameras are also getting smaller, meaning they can be hidden in a wider range of objects.

As that all comes together, there will be a further revolution: cheaper and smaller cameras, remote cameras and flying cameras will open up a number of industries and places that until now have been hidden from view. Covert recording will be more possible anywhere and will be available to anyone. We will all eventually be affected in one way or another. Some of us will be supporting and advising someone who is filming, while others of us will be considering using secret cameras ourselves.

BREAKING OUT OF THE BOX: WIRELESS CAMERAS

The main limiting factor for the types of secret cameras that members of the public use, which tend to be hidden in electronical equipment that can be plugged in, such as smoke alarms or clock radios, has always been that a recorder had to be physically attached to its lens by a cable.[2] As a result, someone has always had to have an object big enough to hide the recorder. The implication is that someone could only film in locations where relatively big objects could both be smuggled in and out without being detected.

That could all be about to change. Wireless minicameras are already widely used in modern 'smart' surveillance systems – where cameras can be monitored from anywhere using a smartphone as long as one has the phone's passcode.

At the moment, my understanding is that people tend to use these cameras in their own homes and businesses. Although there are challenges to be overcome, in future it will be increasingly easy to smuggle a camera lens and transmitter into any number of locations, such as care homes and businesses, hidden in tiny objects. We will see these sorts of remote cameras increasingly used for secret filming and recording, not just open surveillance and monitoring.[3]

As I say, there are real challenges – if these cameras rely on wireless internet connections, then those can be unreliable and transmitting and receiving video footage uses a lot of electricity and bandwidth. Recent advances in both internet and battery technology should mean those difficulties can be overcome – and as more devices transmit automatically, it will be harder to distinguish between a device being used by someone transmitting secret footage and any number of other electrical devices generating signals.

The result, if I am right, is that in the same way miniature lenses cleverly wired up to a small recorder have become available to most anyone, in a short period of time even more clever miniature lenses which don't have to be connected to a recorder will be used by people doing their own secret filming. These lenses can be several rooms – or eventually any distance – away from their recorder. They will become increasingly common.

The limiting factor at the moment with such cameras is only how to get the video from the lens to the recorder. The simplest method is if there is a wireless Internet connection. A camera can piggyback on that network and in effect transmit its footage. Even that kind of issue will be less and less important for remote cameras in future. Some small commercially available cameras already generate their own internet connection – so filming can be monitored at a distance. That will only become more common in future.

The result will be secret filming that can occur almost anywhere. The potential to prevent wrongdoing and protect people from harm will be incredible. Cameras will be remotely managed and monitored – and hidden in places that, at the moment, we cannot imagine. Almost all the same challenges highlighted in this book will still have to be overcome, but the fact that new entities could be held up to scrutiny could be a powerful and important driver for change.

FLYING HECK: DRONE CAMERAS

The other new technology literally hovering just over the horizon is the unmanned drone. American author Adam Rothstein explains:

> Drones available for commercial sale tend to be of quadrotor or other multirotor configuration, which are much cheaper and easier to fly than helicopters, and have slower flight and hover capabilities than fixed-wing aircraft… In quadrotor, two sets of two propellers spin in opposite directions, one set countering the rotational force of the other. By slowly accelerating or decelerating one set of rotors, the craft can yaw and roll side to side.[4]

Little helicopters the size of a small dog can already fly low and safely within civilian airspace. These machines were once the preserve of the military. Smaller, less sophisticated aerial cameras held aloft by eight or more miniature helicopter blades are being used by film crews all over the world as a cheaper alternative to helicopter filming. The online company Amazon is examining delivering express packages without mailmen, instead using a fleet of unmanned drones.

We can expect the sort of aerial covert surveillance that would only have been the preserve of government intelligence agencies to become more common with each passing year. Whereas a worried spouse used to pay a man to 'tail' or follow someone, soon more people will be able to observe someone's door from the air at particular times of day.

The limiting factor on drones is currently the law. There are regulations in the UK (and in many other countries, from what I understand) controlling a number of specific points – for example, how far from other people a drone can take off or land. Other regulations are intended to prevent drones from interfering with aircraft taking off or landing at airports.[5] This is a fast-moving area, and there are already calls for more regulation and control because those rules are being broken.[6]

Some states in the United States have introduced specific laws to tackle surveillance by drones. Adam Rothstein argues that this is excessive, that fear almost of the *concept* of drones is driving a disproportionate response:

> ...we tend to think of a drone as having surveillance capabilities unique among other platforms. In congressional testimony regarding the use of drones in the United States, privacy is brought up as an issue time and again. California passed legislation about the use of data collected by drones in early 2014, and many other states are considering similar laws. And yet there is no similar legislation in the United States about Stingrays, ALPRs [automatic license-plate recognition], CCTV [closed-circuit television] or other similar technologies. Somehow, the invasion of privacy by drones is considered more worthy of regulation, though the technology is very similar.[7]

In future, the concern will be more ethical and less technical as cameras are used more widely and in new settings. The answers will be about ensuring and policing the *use* of covert technology, just as in the past.

I recently attended a model-making exhibition in London where one of the stalls with the longest queue was the drone stand. It seems to me improbable that, in an era when people are increasingly using apps downloaded to their partner's phone to keep an eye on them, we will not see new and inventive used of drones for surveillance as well as for play. A drone is coming soon to a watchful husband, a worried employer or a journalistic investigation near you, I suspect. The danger, as with any new secret filming method, is that such uses could quickly lead to a public backlash, particularly if a drone hurts someone when crashing or causes an accident.

WHAT WILL THESE NEW TECHNOLOGIES AND METHODS MEAN?

Already different countries approach in different ways the challenges and possibilities posed by secret cameras. The appearance of smaller cameras, cheaper cameras, flying cameras and wireless cameras will just pose new problems that different individuals and different nations will have to resolve. How cameras are used in practice is up to us. The mistake is to think that the kit – that is, the lenses and recorders – are the future or the past. They are just the technology. The ubiquity of cameras in mobile or cellular phones and the increased availability of cheap hidden cameras are in themselves value neutral. Taking drones as an example, Adam Rothstein tried to make this point, arguing that there is a decision to be made about how unmanned flying machines are used. The way they are used at the moment is not how they could be used in future:

> Today drones largely only kill people or spy on them. That is what they are designed to do. There could be a future in which they largely help people and are designed primarily for that purpose... We must get there by ethical development of the technology.[8]

The same is true of all covert filming. The choice is ours.

The danger, of course, is that we could create a paranoid surveillance society:

> In the very near future, we would argue, it is not the occasional snapshot that will be of concern but the streaming of real-time, high quality video to potentially billions of strangers over which the subject has little or no control. One can imagine scenarios whereby teachers, beach bathers, train travellers, shop workers or indeed anyone operating in a public space will have to keep in the back of their mind that their activities may be secretly monitored by the pupil, stranger or customer next to them...[9]

Such fears are widespread at the moment. Another expert, Finnish lecturer Agneta Mallén, argues in similar terms that the result will be fewer private spaces:

> ... because of the increasing number of camera phones, and thus prospective citizen journalists, the control network is growing. Critics of surveillance technology argue that the control net has become increasingly intrusive: the mesh of the net has become finer, while the net itself has grown... The mesh becomes even

finer when in principle anyone with a camera phone
can exercise control over their fellows...[10]

As technology advances, it will have greater potential and
pose greater challenges, because

...it is not unreasonable to imagine smaller,
more powerful and cheaper devices with greater
functionality entering the consumer market. These
devices would be capable of observing, tracking,
capturing, and sharing data in a variety of formats
about their environments and the individuals around
them. At this point serious ethical questions begin to
emerge around personal liberty and surveillance.[11]

It does not have to be like that, I would argue. Those sort of
dystopian predictions assume the worst about people's use
of technology: just because people can film everything does
not mean they will.

When members of the public take up cameras in
an ethical fashion to prevent wrongdoing or expose
mistreatment, I do not think it is part of a giant data mesh
that traps us all. In the teeth of growing national and
corporate surveillance, the 'little guy' taking up cameras is
often an act of resistance – a reclamation of cameras not for
control but instead for justice.

I am reminded of the complaints I hear from care
home owners who do not mind the idea of putting up
CCTV cameras themselves in 'their' bedrooms, but who are
horrified that a member of the public could do their own
filming. It seems to me there is something different between
the citizen who takes up cameras in self-defence and the big
company or state swinging its lenses about the place.

All invasion of privacy is not equal. When it is done
by the state or big companies, it has one moral compass,

but perhaps the next generation of citizen journalists using cameras face the same essential ethical position without quite the same dangers. Any one family worried about their relative in a care home, for example, is obviously not trying to construct a super state that deprives us all of our liberty.

FEWER PROFESSIONALS AND MORE 'ORDINARY' PEOPLE DOING THE FILMING

There is a final prediction for the future, the one that is really what has inspired me to write this book and which I'll emphasise one last time: the future of secret filming will be more about members of public using cameras, and less about professionals. As described in Chapter 1 about the history of secret filming, there was a time when journalists appeared to be at the centre of the story of secret filming. People plying my profession produced most of the covert footage that people were likely to see, usually on television. That already is less true, but it is going to be even less true as time passes. In other words, the cameras are passing into the hands of a new generation, and at the same time the decisions about how those cameras should be used will also be in new hands. I hope they choose wisely.

As I've written this book, I've found myself reflecting a lot on the fact that journalists like me *appear* to be important to secret filming, but the truth is that my profession only appears to be important because we make the television programmes people watch. In many ways, the public taking over by doing their own secret filming is really just the snake shedding its skin. All journalists ever are really is mediators – facilitators who enable publication or broadcast to occur. As a profession, we like talking up our accomplishments, but it is always real people who actually suffer or who speak out that are the real heroes.

Even in the nineteenth century when 'Nellie Bly' was reporting on the mistreatment of mentally ill people in New York (see Chapter 4), she only knew there was something to expose because of the brave people who had already spoken out to journalists at her newspaper, warning them what was really going on.

At that time and for the century since, journalists or other professionals, such as social workers or inspectors, have mediated all the big revelations. Someone who sees bad things has needed to 'get someone to do something about it'. Cameras are empowering in a fundamental way. Now those same citizens can do something about it themselves. Technology is removing or reducing the gatekeepers, and the fact that increasingly people are filming evidence for themselves could be and should be a good thing for all of us.

NOTES

1. This is not impossible, though it *is* unlikely (see discussion in Chapter 5 – for example, see pages 63 and 64).

2. As a side point, for professional journalists like me who usually use secret cameras worn on their body or hidden in bags, battery power has been a greater constraint than the presence of a recorder on what objects can be used. However, I have yet to meet a member of the public using secret cameras hidden in either bags or shirts.

3. See, for example, Ferenbok, J. and Clement, A. (2012) Hidden Changes, from CCTV to 'Smart' Video Surveillance. In Doyle, A., Lippert, R. and Lyon, D. (eds) *Eyes Everywhere: The Global Growth of Camera Surveillance* (pp.220–221). London: Routledge.

4. Rothstein, A. (2015) *Drone* (p.36). London: Bloomsbury.

5. For British drone regulations, see http://droneflight.co.uk/pages/summary-of-uk-legal-requirements, accessed on 31 July 2015; or for more details, see www.caa.co.uk/application.aspx?catid=33&pagetype=65&appid=11&mode=detail&id=226, accessed on 31 July 2015.

6. Piggott, R. (2014) 'Heathrow plane in near miss with drone.' Available at www.bbc.co.uk/news/uk-30369701, accessed on 18 December 2014.

7. Rothstein, *op. cit.*, p.78.

8. *Ibid.*, p.144.

9. Saulles de, M. and Horner, D.S. (2011) 'The portable panopticon: Morality and mobile technologies.' *Journal of Information, Communication & Ethics in Society 9*, 3, 209.

10. Mallén, A. (2012) 'Citizen Journalism, Surveillance and Control.' In G.V. Walle, N. Zurawski and E. Van den Herrewegen (eds) (2012) *Crime, Security and Surveillance: Effects for the Surveillant and the Surveilled* (p.9). The Hague: Boom/Eleven International Publishing. Available at www.academia.edu/2416955/Citizen_Journalism_Surveillance_and_Control, accessed on 23 June 2014.

11. Saulles de, M. and Horner, D.S. (2011) 'The portable panopticon: Morality and mobile technologies.' *Journal of Information, Communication & Ethics in Society 9*, 3, 213.

UNDERCOVER TALES

Back to the Future:
Old Problems, New Cameras

The poor, the unlucky and the weak will continue to be preyed upon all over the world unless someone proves unequivocally – with cameras, again and again – what is going on. The oldest problems still remain with us, just in different places and in different ways. Vulnerable adults and children, as well as animals, will always be subject to mistreatment until many more people stand up against that tide. It is a little like that fairground game where no matter how many gophers you strike with a toy mallet, another one just pops up. Each time a major social ill is highlighted or exposed, the problem is just chipped at, not resolved forever.

I have strong feelings about one of the longest-running injustices in the world: the exploitation of people dying of cancer. This last undercover tale concerns my wearing hidden cameras to expose one such case.

The dying and desperate have been sold dirty water and chalk pills, have been poisoned and exploited by people pretending to peddle miracle cures for centuries. In the UK and elsewhere, that is supposed to be outlawed: the British Parliament passed a law making it illegal for anyone who is not a medical doctor to claim to treat cancer. Full stop. No quacks and no fake cures.

Despite that legislation dating back to 1939, the problem has not gone away. It was October 2003, I was in the Midlands. We had pulled over in a service station and the man I was working with, John Inchley, went off for a cigarette. He explained to me that since he'd been diagnosed with incurable cancer, he did not see any reason to abstain. We both had hidden cameras and were on our way to secretly film a man who was not a qualified doctor. He had said he could offer John treatment for his incurable cancer. The man we were going to film, whom I'll call 'Graham', was using an Australian massage device, a short glass tube which sent electric pulses along its length. He had imported one and claimed it could cure cancer. Connected up to one of various small glass tubes, it produces a small amount of purple light, a small amount of warmth and a tiny amount of ozone. The manufacturers do make exalted claims for their product, but even they didn't claim it was a cure for cancer when we contacted them.

I was carrying a camera in my bag, and John was wearing a camera in his top, both hidden, when we arrived at the door of an ordinary suburban house on the edge of a Midland's town. Graham's wife answered the door. Graham was 'attending to another client', she said, so we'd have to wait. It was a simple semi-detached house that felt crowded despite its two floors, with a tiny front hallway and thinly carpeted stairs which led up to a landing, which Graham used – at least with us – as his waiting area for clients.

Graham's main business was as a hypnotherapist, and you could feel it by the way his gaze locked on to yours and his eyes pierced into you. His treatment began without the machine. First he asked John to repeat a series of things that he said:

'Say "I want to be healthy".'

'I want to be healthy.'

'Say it again.'

'I want to be healthy.'

'No, no, watch how I do it. Draw your breath in and with your arms like this [outstretched, curved and then pulled back in] say, "I want to be healthy".'

After interminable mumbo-jumbo, Graham admitted, 'I'm not getting through. You are not letting go. I can tell you are letting your mind get in the way.'

Despite his extreme cynicism, John tried his best. He really gave it his all, repeating whatever Graham said. Then the Australian massage device came out. Both John and I were secretly filming it all. Graham rubbed the glass tube on John's head as it buzzed away.

'So this is going to cure my cancer? By rubbing this on my head I'll get better?'

'In combination with everything else, it will help make you better,' Graham replied.

'How?' John asked.

'You have to let go of your questioning.'

John was basically sold various out-of-date supplements and had an electrical gadget rubbed across his head, but what Graham was really pedalling was something much more intense: hope – false but tempting hope. Real doctors usually tell people in John's condition that they cannot be cured – that they will die. Now Graham was telling him that actually he could be not just treated but made 'better'.

As we walked away from the house, John explained what bothered him most:

> They try to blame the victim. They tell you that it's your fault – that if you just tried hard enough, believed hard enough, bought enough gizmos, you wouldn't die. That's a horrible thing to tell someone who's dying.

Our television programme was broadcast on regional BBC in 2003. John has died now, but we filmed him then saying:

> There are all kinds of strange therapies out there and most of them have no scientific basis. There are people in my position who probably feel little hope and who are prepared to go to any length to effect a cure.[1]

Graham did not invent his procedure. He learned everything he knew about that machine from a guy called Reg Gill. We do not know how many people with cancer Reg and then Graham 'treated', but we did know of one: a man called Stephen Hall. Stephen was a large man, physically impressive but also with a strong character; a performer and serious barbershop chorus singer, conductor and arranger.
As Stephen's cancer progressed, he began emailing and finally speaking with Reg, who claimed that cancer was actually a disease that had to do with tiny microbes leaving one part of the body and travelling to another, and that these malignant bodies could be affected by 'electromagnetic waves'.

Stephen's mother, Sheila Cracknell, remembers that, by the end, even Stephen had his doubts about Reg, and she stated, 'He started saying that maybe he – maybe people –

should take the best from all worlds.' From these words and the look in his eyes, his mother Sheila was clear. She said that Stephen had a look in his eye that suggested he knew Reg was not going to cure him, that Reg had promised more than he could possibly deliver.

In future, I expect that I will increasingly hear from people like John once they have secret footage they have filmed all by themselves. Most of the issues families and citizen journalists will tackle with secret cameras will be the same fundamental injustices others have faced before. Social problems can change, inequities can be righted, but it will take luck, strength of will and real caution from those who use hidden cameras in future.

Good luck to them – and to all those who support them.

NOTE

1. BBC (2003) 'Quack medicine.' Available at www.bbc.co.uk/insideout/south.series2/quack_medicine_alternative_cancer_cures.shtml, accessed on 22 October 2015.